LIFE MANAGEMENT SKILLS II

reproducible activity handouts created for facilitators

A sampler collection of...

activities of daily living
anger management
assertion
communication: verbal
communication: nonverbal
coping skills
grief / loss
humor
life balance

money management
parenting
reminiscence
safety issues
self-esteem / self-image
steps to recovery
stress management
support systems
time management

Kathy L. Korb, OTR/L   Stacey D. Azok, OTR/L   Estelle A. Leutenberg

WELLNESS REPRODUCTIONS
INCORPORATED

This book is dedicated to our families...
for their never-ending patience and words of encouragement,
for their time and flexibility, and for their ongoing support
throughout the past year of writing and creating
Life Management Skills II.

THANK YOU to... Ya'akov, Shayna, Arielle, and Mason;
to Frank and Hannah; and to Jay, Lynne, and Amy.
We love and appreciate you all!

SPECIAL THANKS TO...

Patricia Clarkson

Mimi Dragicevich, OTR

Michele Guerrieri

Nan Hooley

Sgt. Joe Iliano

Georgette Kashawlic

Erwin M. Leffel, Coordinator
  of Chemical Abuse Program,
  Willoughby-Eastlake City Schools

Gary S. Okin, JD

Bonny Reed, COTA/L
Barberton Citizens Hospital

B.J. and Julian Udelson, PhD

Diane Wetzig, PhD, CAS

Willoughby-Eastlake City
Schools CORE Team

Mae R. Zelikow

Heights Negative & Plate Staff

Thanks to the therapists, counselors, educators and all those who provided us with
feedback and encouragement to write Life Management Skills II.

THANKS TO OUR ILLUSTRATOR...

Amy Leutenberg

Amy L. Leutenberg graduated from Kent State University with a B.A. in Art Education and a B.F.A. in Studio Art. She currently works in a residential facility for emotionally-disturbed children, continues to pursue her career as an artist, and is enrolled in the Master's program at the Mandel School of Applied Social Sciences at Case Western Reserve University.

FOREWORD

The inspiration for our LIFE MANAGEMENT SKILLS books originated from an ongoing practical need observed within a mental health setting. Handouts had been typically used in treatment as a launching pad for activities, an organizational tool, a visual aid, a tangible reminder of information presented, and as a method for building rapport. However, available handouts often did not meet necessary, high-quality standards in content desired, format, appearance, and organization — and lacked permission for reproduction.

We have attempted to meet these standards by offering this sampler collection of handouts which are highly reproducible, organized in a logical manner, designed for specific well-defined purposes, and activity-based, allowing for extensive client involvement. The graphic representations are intentionally different from handout to handout in typestyle, art, and design to increase visual appeal, provide variety, and clarify meaning.

LIFE MANAGEMENT SKILLS handouts are adaptable and have a broad usage enabling therapists, social workers, nurses, teachers, psychologists, counselors, and other professionals to focus on specific goals with their specific populations.

The book has been designed to offer reproducible handouts on the front of each page and nonreproducible facilitator's information on the reverse side. The Facilitator's Information Sheet includes the following sections: Purpose, General Comments, and Possible Activities.

We specifically chose spiral binding to allow for easier and accurate reproduction, an especially white paper for clear, sharp copies, and a heavier paper stock for its durability and opacity. If adaptations to any of the handouts are desired, it is recommended to make one copy of the handout, include the changes which will meet *your* specific needs, and then use this copy as the original.

We hope that you will find these handouts in LIFE MANAGEMENT SKILLS II fun, innovative, and informative. We wish you much success with your therapeutic and educational endeavors and hope we can continue to be of assistance. Remember... creative handouts will hopefully generate creative activities and contribute to a greater sense of WELLNESS!

Wellness Reproductions Inc.

Kathy L. Korb   *Stacey D. Azok*   *Estelle A. Leutenberg*

Wellness Reproductions Inc. is an innovative company which began in 1988, by Kathy L. Korb, OTR/L, Stacey D. Azok, OTR/L, and Estelle A. Leutenberg. As developers of creative therapeutic and educational products, we have a strong commitment to the mental health profession. Our rapidly growing business began by authoring and self-publishing the book LIFE MANAGEMENT SKILLS. We have extended our product line to include group presentation posters, a therapeutic board game, the school-based curriculum SEALS program (Self-Esteem and Life Skills), an annual NET·WORK·SHOP, and now, another book, LIFE MANAGEMENT SKILLS II. This book was created with feedback from our customers. Please refer to the last page of this book, our "FEEDBACK" page, and let us hear from YOU!

TABLE OF CONTENTS

Page numbers are on the Facilitator's Information Sheet, located on the reverse side of each handout.

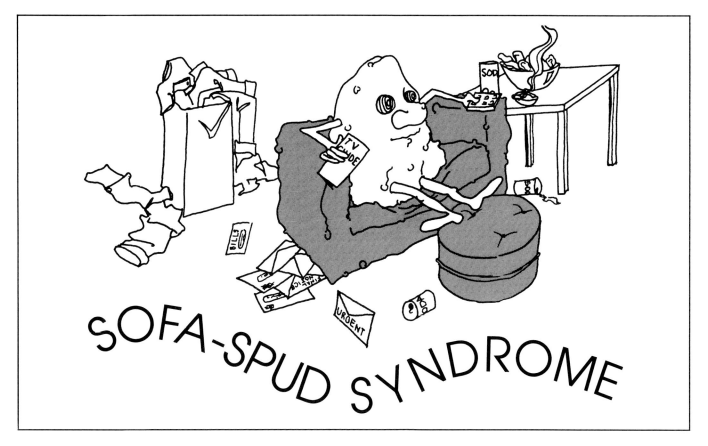

SOFA-SPUD SYNDROME

1.) DO YOU HAVE TROUBLE GETTING UP AND LEAVING A COMFORTABLE PLACE?

2.) DO YOU SIT FOR ENDLESS HOURS IN ONE PLACE WITH NO "GET UP AND GO"?

3.) DO YOU HAVE MORE JUNK FOODS OR DRINKS THAN NUTRITIOUS FOODS?

4.) ARE THE BILLS, LAUNDRY AND DISHES PILING UP?

5.) ARE THE TELEVISION GUIDE AND REMOTE CONTROL YOUR <u>BEST FRIENDS</u>?

6.) IS THE BATHROOM BECOMING A <u>FOREIGN PLACE</u>?

1.) _____ 2.) _____ 3.) _____ 4.) _____ 5.) _____ 6.) _____

IF YOU ANSWERED <u>YES</u> TO 2 OR MORE OF THE ABOVE SYMPTOMS, YOU HAVE THE DREADED...
SOFA-SPUD SYNDROME. ALL KIDDING ASIDE, THE SOFA-SPUD SYNDROME HAS PRETTY
SERIOUS IMPLICATIONS: **POOR PHYSICAL AND MENTAL HEALTH!**

TRY ANSWERING THESE QUESTIONS TO HELP YOU MAKE A PLAN:

What can I *say to myself* to give me that "get up and go"? _____

What helps motivate me? _____

What limits can I put on my behavior? _____

What is one activity I can do after I "get up and go"? _____

Who can support me to "get up and go"? _____

Other ideas: _____

_____

SET A GOAL TODAY — MASH SOFA-SPUD SYNDROME!

SOFA-SPUD SYNDROME!

I. PURPOSE:

To increase awareness of compromised activities of daily living (ADLs).

To problem-solve methods which promote higher functioning in ADLs.

II. GENERAL COMMENTS:

Lethargy impairs *all* occupational performance areas:
   work,
   self-care,
   and leisure,
however self-care skills are often compromised *first*.

The SOFA-SPUD SYNDROME is a light-hearted way to approach declining ADLs.

III. POSSIBLE ACTIVITIES:

A. 1. Distribute handouts.

   2. Facilitate a discussion of symptoms listed, as well as group members' own symptoms of SOFA-SPUD SYNDROME.

   3. Problem-solve methods to promote higher functioning in ADLs.

   4. Discuss issues with each group member stating one daily goal.

   5. Process effects that ADLs have on self-esteem, self-confidence and self-image.

B. 1. Distribute handouts.

   2. Facilitate discussion of SOFA-SPUD SYNDROME.

   3. Make 4 photocopies of the questions (under "TRY ANSWERING . . .") from the lower portion of the handout, and cut six strips (one question per strip). You now have 24 questions to place in basket.

   4. Pass basket to all group members so that each person takes one question (2 questions may be chosen if group is small and time allows).

   5. Encourage turn-taking as group members read their questions aloud and respond accordingly.

   6. Assist each group member to state response in terms of a concrete, short-term goal.

   7. Process benefits of this activity.

Activities of Daily Living

DATE:

NAME:

ACTIVITY	DAILY	WEEKLY	NEED TO CHANGE NOW	PRIORITIZE
★ bathe				
★ brush teeth/oral care				
★ eat nutritiously				
★ exercise				
★ shave				
★ apply makeup/aftershave/cologne				
★ wash hair				
★ apply deodorant				
★ take medications/vitamins				
★ comb/brush hair				
★ care for nails				
★				
• wash clothes/towels/etc.				
• wash dishes				
• prepare meals				
• pay bills				
• straighten up room/apartment/house				
• make bed				
• change linens				
• clean house				
• shop for groceries/personal items				
• maintain yard/property				
• repair household items				
•				

GOALS   GOALS   GOALS   GOALS   GOALS

Activities of Daily Living

I. PURPOSE:

To increase independence in activities of daily living (ADLs).

II. GENERAL COMMENTS:

ADLs refer to the skill and performance of self-care, work, and leisure activities. *This* handout focuses on personal health and home management. Symptoms of depression such as lethargy, low motivation and poor initiative are just a few factors preventing higher or more independent functioning in ADLs. Recognizing specific areas of deficit, prioritizing them, and setting goals will improve independence in these areas. Information from this activity might be valuable as an assessment tool or in progress notes.

III. POSSIBLE ACTIVITIES:

A. 1. Distribute handout as an assessment tool or activity for a one-to-one or group session.

   2. Complete the handouts with individuals or group members as follows:

      a. Read list of ADL tasks. Add other significant tasks.

      b. In column 1, DAILY, write amount of times performed daily, e.g., bathe 1 time.

      c. In column 2, WEEKLY, write amount of times performed in a one week period, e.g., change linens 1 time.

      d. In column 3, NEED TO CHANGE NOW, review columns 1 & 2 and indicate with a check mark if there is a need to change the behavior now. (There may be one or more checks.)

      e. In column 4, PRIORITIZE, review column 3 and prioritize the areas checked. Rank in order of importance: #1, #2 and #3.

   3. Discuss why they are a priority: effects on self-esteem, self-confidence, self-image, relationships, work and leisure.

   4. Develop a plan and write goals (for handouts on Goal Setting, see Life Management Skills, Book 1, pages 36, 37 and 38. Order form on last page of this book).

   5. Process benefits of activity.

   6. Provide follow-up as necessary, updating goals.

B. 1. Distribute handout as an assessment tool or activity for a one-to-one or group session.

   2. Complete the handouts with individuals or group members as follows:

      a. Read list of ADL tasks. Add other significant tasks.

      b. In column 1, DAILY, write amount of times performed daily, e.g., bathe 1 time.

      c. In column 2, WEEKLY, write amount of times performed in a one week period, e.g., change linens 1 time.

      d. In column 3, NEED TO CHANGE NOW, review columns 1 & 2 and indicate with a check mark if there is a need to change the behavior now. (There may be one or more checks.)

      e. In column 4, PRIORITIZE, review column 3 and prioritize the areas checked. Rank in order of importance: #1, #2 and #3.

   3. Divide group into 2 subgroups, according to common deficits, in the areas of 1) personal health (★) and 2) home management (•). Within subgroups, encourage discussion of specific areas of deficits (i.e. exercise, prepare meals), options, and possible solutions. Promote group support and feedback in goal setting.

   4. Reconvene group and encourage each group member to read his/her goal aloud.

   5. Process benefits of activity.

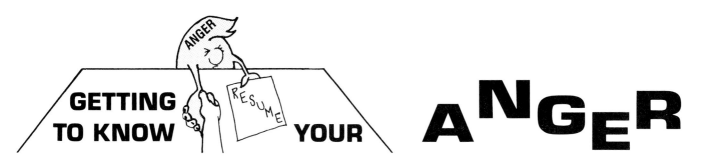

GETTING TO KNOW YOUR ANGER

Anger is a normal, human emotion. It is intense. Everyone gets angry and has a right to his/her anger. The trick is managing your anger effectively so that it will mobilize you in POSITIVE, not negative, directions.

The first step in **ANGER MANAGEMENT** is to get to know your anger by recognizing its symptoms.

DO YOU . . .

physical	emotional	behavioral

__ grit your teeth?

__ get a headache?

__ get sweaty palms?

__ get dizzy?

__ get red-faced?

__ get a stomachache?

__ feel like running away?

__ get depressed?

__ feel guilty?

__ feel resentment?

__ become anxious?

__ feel like lashing out?

__ cry/yell/scream?

__ use substances?

__ get sarcastic?

__ lose sense of humor?

__ become abusive?

__ withdraw?

__ _____

__ _____

__ _____

__ _____

__ _____

__ _____

DOES YOUR ANGER . . .

__ last too long?

__ become too intense?

__ lead to aggression?

__ impair relationships?

__ interfere with major roles? (parent, worker, student)

__ creep out in mysterious ways?

__ contribute to physical problems?

__ come too frequently?

__ flare up too quickly?

__ _____

__ _____

__ _____

ANGER INVENTORY (Rate 1-5) Rank your anger in the following situations.

1-no annoyance	2-little irritated	3-upset	4-quite angry	5-very angry

__ You've overheard people joking about you or your family.

__ You're not being treated with respect or consideration.

__ You're singled out for corrections while the actions of others go unnoticed.

__ You're hounded by a salesperson from the moment you walk into a store.

__ You're trying to discuss something important with someone, who isn't giving you a chance to talk or express your feelings.

__ Someone offers continual, unsolicited advice.

__ You're in a discussion with someone who persists in arguing about a topic s/he knows very little about.

__ You've had a busy day and the person you live with greets you with complaints about what you haven't finished.

__ Someone is given special consideration because of his/her popularity, good looks, financial position, or family status.

__ Someone comments on your being overweight/underweight.

__ **TOTAL**

Additional situations that spark YOUR anger.

_____

_____

_____

...perhaps it's time to work on your anger management skills!

I. PURPOSE:

To increase knowledge and awareness of physical, behavioral and emotional anger symptoms.

II. GENERAL COMMENTS:

Oftentimes, anger is misunderstood and unrecognized. "Getting to know your anger" and confronting it is the first step in effective anger management.

III. POSSIBLE ACTIVITIES:

A. 1. Distribute handouts and review. When discussing "anger inventory", ask group members to share their totals. Remind group members that unmanaged anger will have a negative effect on physical and mental health.

   2. Instruct group members to write anger vertically 3 times on the back of each handout.

      A   A   A
      N   N   N
      G   G   G
      E   E   E
      R   R   R

   3. Ask that group members use the first set of letters to describe their physical anger symptoms in words or phrases, e.g.,

        A - aches
        N - nausea
        G - gritting teeth
        E - energy loss
        R - rigid posture

   4. Continue using the second set for emotional symptoms, e.g.,

        A - anxious
        N - negative
        G - guilty
        E - embarrassed
        R - resentful

   5. And the third set for behavioral anger symptoms, e.g.,

        A - alcohol
        N - narcotics, nicotine
        G - getting into trouble
        E - eat a lot
        R - risk - safety

   6. Encourage sharing of group members' responses by listing them on the chalkboard.

   7. Process benefits of increased awareness of personal anger symptoms.

B. 1. Distribute handouts and review. When discussing "anger inventory", ask group members to share their totals. Remind group members that unmanaged anger will have a negative effect on physical and mental health.

   2. Complete handouts.

   3. Direct group members into pairs for sharing of responses. Allot time for both partners to share in detail (approximately 15-20 minutes).

   4. Return to large group and give each group member 1-2 minutes to summarize his/her partner's anger profile. Encourage feedback from others as appropriate.

   5. Process benefits of this activity.

ANGER STYLES

☑ STUFFING   ☐ ESCALATING   ☐ MANAGING

Do you "stuff" your anger? _____

Do you tend to avoid direct confrontation? _____

"Stuffers" can deny anger...
> *they may not admit to themselves or to others that they are angry.*

"Stuffers" may not be aware that they have the <u>right</u> to be angry.

Some reasons we "stuff" are:

1] fear of hurting/offending someone. ☐

2] fear of being disliked or rejected. ☐

3] fear of losing control. ☐

4] feeling it's inappropriate (not ok) to be angry. ☐

5] feeling unable to cope with such a strong, intense emotion. ☐

6] fear of damaging/losing a relationship. ☐

7] it's a learned behavior (but, it can be unlearned!). ☐

8] trying to use a different style than the one I was raised with. ☐

9] _____

10] _____

Consequences/Problems:

1] anger comes out — regardless.

2] impairs relationships.

3] compromises physical and mental health.

4] _____

5] _____

WELCOME!

I. PURPOSE:

To increase knowledge of the anger style called "stuffing".

To identify personal anger styles.

II. GENERAL COMMENTS:

"Stuffing" describes the passive style of coping with anger. Being able to identify a personal anger style is an early step in anger management.

III. POSSIBLE ACTIVITIES: This handout can be used in conjunction with ANGER STYLES - ESCALATING (page 5), ANGER STYLES - MANAGING I (page 6), and ANGER STYLES - MANAGING II (page 7).

A. 1. Distribute handouts.

2. Discuss, encouraging group members to offer comments regarding this anger style.

3. Attempt to list T.V./movie/book/cartoon characters, historical figures, and occupations that demonstrate the "stuffing" style.

4. Introduce the ANGER STYLES - ESCALATING page.

5. Introduce ANGER STYLES - MANAGING pages as a more effective style.

6. Process problems associated with the "stuffing" style and benefits of "managing".

B. 1. Review topic of "stuffing" briefly.

2. Encourage each group member to share a situation in which s/he "stuffed" anger, why, and consequences resulting.

3. Distribute handouts and complete as a group, recalling prior discussion.

4. Discuss benefits of greater self-awareness and ask each group member to set a short-term goal to learn effective anger management skills.

ANGER STYLES

☐ **STUFFING** ☑ **ESCALATING** ☐ **MANAGING**

Do you "escalate" to rage? _____

Do you try to control, but lose control? _____

"Escalators" blame and shame the "provoker".

"Escalating" often leads to abusive situations.

Some reasons we escalate are:

1] feeling "I have no other choice". ☐

2] to demonstrate an image of strength/power. ☐

3] to avoid expressing underlying emotions. ☐

4] fear of getting close to someone. ☐

5] it's a learned behavior (but, it can be unlearned!). ☐

6] lack of communication skills. ☐

7] _____

8] _____

Consequences/Problems:

1] desired results may be short-term.

2] possible physical destruction.

3] impairs relationships.

4] compromises physical and mental health.

5] legal ramifications.

6] _____

7] _____

I. PURPOSE:

To increase knowledge of the anger style called "escalating".

To identify personal anger styles.

II. GENERAL COMMENTS:

"Escalating" describes the aggressive style of coping with anger. Being able to identify a personal anger style is an early step in anger management.

III. POSSIBLE ACTIVITIES: This handout can be used in conjunction with ANGER STYLES - STUFFING (page 4), ANGER STYLES - MANAGING I (page 6), and ANGER STYLES - MANAGING II (page 7)

A. 1. Distribute handouts.

2. Discuss, encouraging group members to offer comments regarding this anger style.

3. Attempt to list T.V./movie/book/cartoon characters, historical figures, and occupations that demonstrate the "escalating" style.

4. Introduce the ANGER STYLES - STUFFING page.

5. Introduce ANGER STYLES - MANAGING pages as a more effective style.

6. Process problems associated with the "escalating" style and benefits of managing.

B. 1. Review topic of "escalating" briefly.

2. Encourage each group member to share a situation in which s/he "escalated" to anger, why, and consequences resulting.

3. Distribute handouts and complete as a group, recalling prior discussion.

4. Discuss benefits of greater self-awareness and ask each group member to set a short-term goal to learn effective anger management skills.

ANGER STYLES

☐ **STUFFING**   ☐ **ESCALATING**   ☑ **MANAGING I**

I'm really working hard on managing my anger — so . . . I need to talk to you. I feel angry when . . .

Do you "manage" your anger?_____

Do you allow anger to mobilize you in positive directions? _____

OPEN, HONEST AND DIRECT EXPRESSION is the most effective way of managing anger.
Easier said than done, huh? When expressing anger directly, keep these important skills in mind . . .

- Remind yourself that anger is a normal, human emotion — it's OK to feel angry!
- Before *open, honest and direct expression*, evaluate the following —
    What was the trigger event?   Is this good timing for the listener?
- Set a specific time limit for anger discussion.
- Remember your body language —
    firm voice — moderate tone — direct eye contact —
    maintain personal "space" — establish an even eye level with the listener
- Don't attack or blame the person.
- Focus on the specific behavior that triggered your anger.
- Avoid *black and white* thinking. ("You never . . . ").
    Instead, "I'd prefer that . . . , then I would feel . . . "
- Use "I" statements.
    "I" feel angry when . . . "   "I" feel angry that . . . "
- Avoid statements/actions that you'll regret later.
- Don't drag in old issues now.
- Check for possible compromises.
- After *open, honest and direct expression*, close the discussion, and then move on!
- _____
- _____
- _____
- When it's over, pat yourself on the back for your assertiveness!
- Say to yourself "I (and perhaps the people around me) will be better off in the long run!"

NOW say to yourself —
    "By managing my anger I took an important step in improving my sense of well-being!"

ANGER STYLES
STUFFING   ESCALATING   ✓ MANAGING I

I. PURPOSE:

To increase knowledge of the anger style called "managing".

To identify personal anger styles.

II. GENERAL COMMENTS.

Managing anger is the most effective method in coping with anger situations. Managing anger by *open, honest and direct expression* is the most effective, yet challenging method. For many, this assertive approach takes effort, energy, time and practice.

III. POSSIBLE ACTIVITIES: This handout can be used in conjunction with ANGER STYLES - STUFFING (page 4), ANGER STYLES - ESCALATING (page 5), and/or ANGER STYLES - MANAGING II (page 7)

A. 1. Distribute handouts following discussion of "stuffing" and "escalating".

    2. Provide discussion, explanation, demonstration, role-plays, etc. of this anger management technique that would benefit the specific population.

    3. Process benefits of *open, honest and direct expression* of anger.

B. 1. Distribute handouts and review.

    2. Instruct all group members to write one anger-provoking situation on a strip of paper and place in a hat.

    3. Facilitate role-plays as each group member chooses one situation from the hat.

    4. During role-play, encourage group members to follow offered guidelines for effective anger management.

    5. Process benefits of *open, honest and direct expression* of anger.

ANGER STYLES

☐ **STUFFING**   ☐ **ESCALATING**   ☑ **MANAGING II**

Do you "manage" your anger? _____
Do you allow anger to mobilize you in positive directions? _____

OPEN, HONEST AND DIRECT EXPRESSION is the most effective way of managing anger.
[see Anger Styles - Managing I]

STUFFING
ESCALATING
MANAGING
Increase daily energy level
Develops effective communication skills
Strengthens relationships
Improves physical and mental health
Boosts self-esteem

3] using the "empty chair" exercise.
Pretend you're sitting across from the person you're angry with and say what's on your mind.
Who is that person? _____

4] writing a letter to the person you're angry with.
You could describe your anger right now, at the time of the anger event or both. You can destroy it/you can save it/you can mail it at a later date.

5] using relaxation techniques.
Guided imagery.
Self-help tapes.
Music.
_____

6] using positive self-talk.
"I am able to choose my anger style."
"I am angry but I'm not going to let it _____
_____."

7] working towards anger resolution through acceptance (learning to live with the fact that certain people and situations, past, present & future, will not change).
Make realistic expectations:
What is one frustrating anger situation? _____
_____
Can it really change as you'd like it to in the near future?
☐ Yes   ☐ No
If not...
• realize the powerlessness over the situation.
• give yourself a time limit to be angry, and then... let it go... !
• constantly remind yourself "I cannot afford to stay angry. What's at stake here?"
• recognize the need for forgiveness.
"No painful event is allowed to contribute to my anger more than one time."
• focus on the present.

Additional effective anger management techniques are:

1] choosing constructive (not destructive) methods/ solutions/ideas.
A. Trying physical outlets.
e.g. exercise, housework, crafts, etc.
_____

B. Problem solving and coming up with action plans.
e.g. forming a neighborhood watch to combat vandalism.
_____

2] involving an objective third party.
Ask someone you trust to be a sounding board.
Who might this be? _____

8] _____
_____
_____

I. PURPOSE:

To increase knowledge of the anger style called "managing".

To identify personal anger styles.

II. GENERAL COMMENTS:

Managing anger is the most effective method in coping with anger situations. This assertive approach offers many effective techniques.

III. POSSIBLE ACTIVITIES: This handout can be used in conjunction with ANGER STYLES - STUFFING (page 4), ANGER STYLES - ESCALATING (page 5), and/or ANGER STYLES - MANAGING I (page 7).

A. 1. Distribute handouts.

2. Provide discussion, explanation, demonstration, role-plays, etc. of the anger management techniques that would benefit the specific population.

3. Process benefits of the "management" style.

B. 1. Instruct all group members to write three anger-provoking situations on separate pieces of paper and place in a hat.

2. Distribute handouts and review.

3. Divide group into smaller subgroups and instruct each subgroup to choose three situations from the hat.

4. Instruct each subgroup to identify two effective "management" techniques from the handout that would assist with each of the anger situations chosen from the hat. Allow 15-20 minutes to complete a written summary of their ideas.

5. Return to large group and have a representative from each subgroup share their summary.

6. Process benefits of activity.

ANGER DIARY

DATE & TIME	
FIRST SYMPTOM(S):	
WHAT TRIGGERED YOUR ANGER RESPONSE?	
YOUR RESPONSE:	
+ / −	
WHAT WAS SOMETHING YOU DID WELL IN THIS SITUATION?	
IS THERE SOMETHING YOU CAN DO IN THE FUTURE TO BETTER MANAGE YOUR ANGER? WHAT?	

ANGER DIARY

I. PURPOSE:

To increase anger management skills by observing, recording and evaluating key events surrounding anger situations.

II. GENERAL COMMENTS:

Anger situations often happen quickly, preventing accurate assessments of details and possible patterns. Diaries assist in the assessment process by allowing the individual to recall key events (some of which may be unpleasant), to record them in a logical, organized way, and later to evaluate them.

III. POSSIBLE ACTIVITIES:

A. 1. Provide handouts and a brief description of the purpose of diaries.

2. Elicit examples of anger situations from group members.

3. Choose one and proceed using the diary format.

4. Process benefits of using a diary to increase anger management skills.

B. 1. Distribute handouts and provide overview of anger diary.

2. Give three strips of paper to each group member and instruct them to write one anger-provoking situation on each. Put all papers into a basket.

3. Pass basket and encourage each group member to choose one strip of paper.

4. Ask each group member to read aloud the situation and offer possible symptoms associated with it, possible responses (positive and negative), specific things done well, and which could be managed better in the future.

5. Encourage group members to identify which situations they have written and insights gained from group activity.

6. Encourage ongoing use of diary to monitor own anger management skills and periodic discussion of diary with others for feedback.

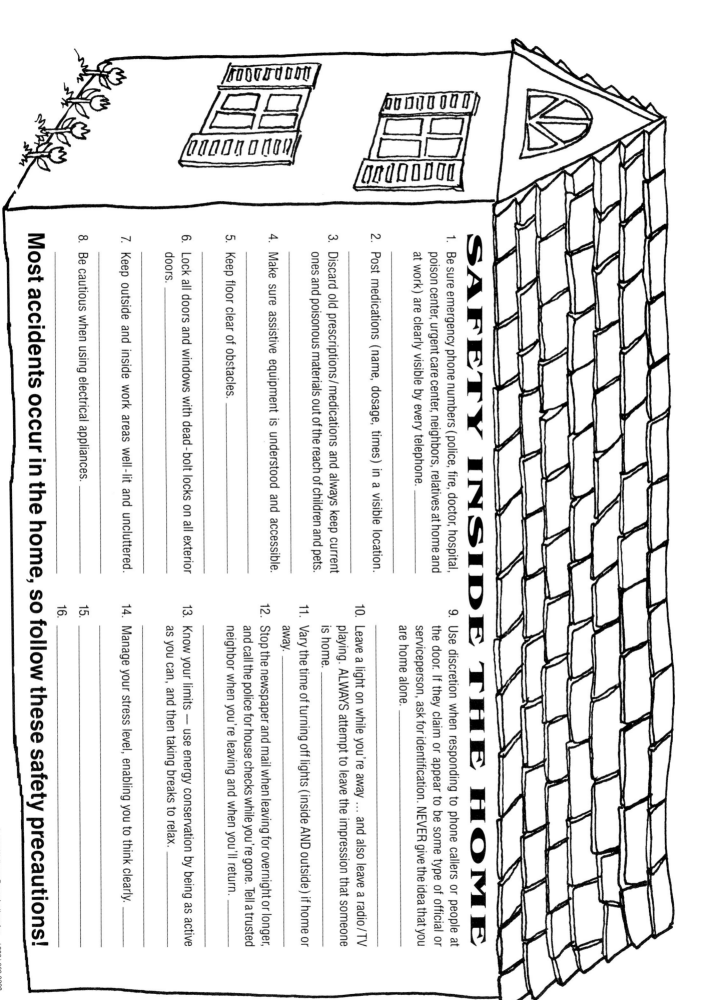

SAFETY INSIDE THE HOME

1. Be sure emergency phone numbers (police, fire, doctor, hospital, poison center, urgent care center, neighbors, relatives at home and at work) are clearly visible by every telephone. _____

2. Post medications (name, dosage, times) in a visible location. _____

3. Discard old prescriptions / medications and always keep current ones and poisonous materials out of the reach of children and pets.

4. Make sure assistive equipment is understood and accessible.

5. Keep floor clear of obstacles. _____

6. Lock all doors and windows with dead - bolt locks on all exterior doors. _____

7. Keep outside and inside work areas well-lit and uncluttered.

8. Be cautious when using electrical appliances. _____

9. Use discretion when responding to phone callers or people at the door. If they claim or appear to be some type of official or serviceperson, ask for identification. NEVER give the idea that you are home alone. _____

10. Leave a light on while you're away … and also leave a radio / TV playing. ALWAYS attempt to leave the impression that someone is home. _____

11. Vary the time of turning off lights (inside AND outside) if home or away. _____

12. Stop the newspaper and mail when leaving for overnight or longer, and call the police for house checks while you're gone. Tell a trusted neighbor when you're leaving and when you'll return. _____

13. Know your limits — use energy conservation by being as active as you can, and then taking breaks to relax. _____

14. Manage your stress level, enabling you to think clearly. _____

15. _____

16. _____

Most accidents occur in the home, so follow these safety precautions!

SAFETY INSIDE THE HOME

I. PURPOSE:

To increase awareness of situations inside the home that require safety measures.

To increase safety skills inside the home.

II. GENERAL COMMENTS:

Most accidents occur in the home. Caution needs to be observed to help prevent accidents in the home, and to reduce chances of burglaries, thefts and vandalism.

III. POSSIBLE ACTIVITIES: This handout can be used in conjunction with SAFETY OUTSIDE THE HOME (page 37).

A. 1. Distribute handouts.

2. Encourage group members to discuss each point by offering explanations/examples from their personal lives.

SOME EXAMPLES INCLUDE:

3   All medicines are to be kept in safety containers and in the medicine cabinet. Poisonous materials are to be kept out of reach and could include: perfumes, cosmetics, paint, household cleaners, soaps/detergents, bug sprays, weed killers.

4   Assistive devices: mount fire extinguisher in kitchen, workshop and garage.

6   Sliding glass doors can be safer with a wooden dowel in the door track.

9   Use discretion with answering machine. Never put your name on the message or let on that you are not at home. Begin message with your telephone number and state that you will return call.

#11   Use automatic timers for lights or have neighbors turn lights on/off at varying times.

#12   When leaving for overnight, have family members or neighbors park their cars in your driveway.

3. Encourage group members to take notes on provided lines.

4. Process benefits of highlighting safety tips.

B. 1. Brainstorm ideas on the chalkboard of ways to increase "safety inside the home".

2. Prepare card game by writing each of the following words on separate cards:
BEDROOM, KITCHEN, LIVING ROOM, BATHROOM, GARAGE, MEDICATION, ELECTRICAL, EQUIPMENT, BASEMENT.

3. Divide group into subgroups of 3-4.

4. Give each subgroup 2-4 cards and encourage them to list ideas of how to increase safety inside the home with regards to...

5. Reconvene as a large group and ask 1 representative from each subgroup to share his/her list.

6. Process benefits of highlighting safety tips.

ASSERTION diary

OPPORTUNITY TO BE ASSERTIVE	MY RESPONSE	FEELINGS AS A RESULT OF MY RESPONSE	WAS I SATISFIED WITH MY RESPONSE?	OTHER POSSIBLE ASSERTIVE RESPONSES
			☐ Yes ☐ Somewhat ☐ No	
			☐ Yes ☐ Somewhat ☐ No	
			☐ Yes ☐ Somewhat ☐ No	
			☐ Yes ☐ Somewhat ☐ No	
			☐ Yes ☐ Somewhat ☐ No	

ASSERTION *diary*

I. PURPOSE:

To increase assertive skills by observing, recording, and evaluating responses in various situations.

To identify alternative assertive responses.

II. GENERAL COMMENTS:

Assertive skills allow for more effective communication. On a daily basis, one is given numerous opportunities to be assertive. Some interactions are handled assertively, thereby enhancing relationships and positively affecting self-esteem; others are handled in a passive or aggressive way, possibly harming relationships and lowering self-esteem. Diaries assist in the assessment process by allowing the individual to 1) recall interactions throughout the day, 2) record them in a logical, organized way, 3) evaluate them, and 4) identify alternative responses.

III. POSSIBLE ACTIVITIES:

A. 1. Provide overview of assertion, discussing how it improves communication and relationships.

2. Distribute handout and provide the following example for group members:

Opportunity To Be Assertive	My Response	Feelings as a Result	Was I Satisfied?	Other Possible Assertive Responses
When the receptionist at the doctor's office continued a personal phone call for several minutes while I was waiting to be assisted.	I said nothing. I just stood there waiting.	Angry. Frustrated. Resentful. Irritated.	☐ yes ☐ somewhat ☒ no	"Excuse me. I have an appointment at 2:00 and would like to fill out any forms while I'm waiting." "Hi, I'm here for my 2:00 appointment and wanted to let you know."

3. Encourage group members to complete handout with 5 examples that have occurred within the past week.

4. Ask group members to share 2-3 of their examples, as time permits, and encourage feedback and support from others.

5. Process benefits of using a diary to increase assertive skills.

B. 1. Photocopy 7 handouts per group member and staple in packets.

2. Provide overview of assertion, discussing how it improves communication and relationships. Include a discussion of the many opportunities available for assertion each day. Briefly describe purpose of diary and benefits.

3. Distribute one packet per group member.

4. Instruct group members to complete the first diary handout for today.

5. Share as able.

6. Instruct group members to use remaining 6 sheets as daily diaries. If possible, follow through in next week's group or individual sessions.

7. Process benefits of using a diary to increase assertive skills.

I HAVE THE RIGHT TO CHANGE A SITUATION.

I WILL EXPLORE OPTIONS & RESPECT MY CHOICES.

SITUATION:
_____
_____

CHANGE:

A. _____
_____

B. _____
_____

C. _____
_____

SITUATION:
_____
_____

CHANGE:

A. _____
_____

B. _____
_____

C. _____
_____

SITUATION:
_____
_____

CHANGE:

A. _____
_____

B. _____
_____

C. _____
_____

I AM ABLE TO FEEL BETTER ABOUT MYSELF
AS I CONSIDER THESE

RIGHT TO CHANGE

I. PURPOSE:

To increase assertive skills by recognizing the right to change a situation.

To identify specific areas of potential change.

II. GENERAL COMMENTS:

Oftentimes, people in crisis think they have no choices. It takes time and effort to confront difficult situations and consider changes.

III. POSSIBLE ACTIVITIES:

A. 1. Provide the following example:

   SITUATION: My spouse doesn't allow me to handle any money.

   CHANGE: A. I can work part-time and receive my own paycheck.
             B. I can ask him/her for $20 a week to manage on my own.
             C. I can take a class on money management at the junior college.

   2. Distribute handouts and encourage group members to complete.

   3. Ask a volunteer to share his/her work with the group, eliciting feedback and assistance to complete handout if needed. Encourage the individual to choose the best option.

   4. Process benefits of recognizing the right to change a situation and identifying specific areas of potential change.

B. 1. Discuss topic of the assertive right to change a situation.

   2. Brainstorm on chalkboard possible situations or areas in need of change.

   FOR EXAMPLE: a) job   f) living arrangements
                     b) money   g) appearance
                     c) friends   h) personality
                     d) family   i) pace of living
                     e) intimate relationships   j) environment

   3. Divide group into subgroups of three members each, and provide each subgroup with one copy of handout.

   4. Instruct each subgroup to choose one category of change listed on chalkboard (refer to examples in B.2.).

   5. Encourage each subgroup to work together to identify three situations within their category which need change (each member needs to contribute one situation). Encourage subgroup members to assist each other in listing possible ways to change each situation. Allow 15-20 minutes.

   6. Reconvene as large group and share responses.

   7. Process benefits of recognizing the right to change a situation and identifying specific areas of potential change. Process benefits of eliciting support from others when deciding on changes.

Self-Disclosure

Complete the following statements to gain an increased understanding of your SELF. You may want to DISCLOSE these thoughts and feelings to someone special to enhance your relationship.

· I am most content when _____
_____

· My hopes and dreams for the future are _____
_____

· I like myself most when _____
_____

· I like myself least when _____
_____

· My greatest fear is _____
_____

· I feel disappointed when _____
_____

· People think I am _____
_____

· I value most _____
_____

· One negative trait about myself is _____
_____

· One positive trait about myself is _____
_____

I'm going to share these thoughts and feelings with _____.

Self-Disclosure

I. PURPOSE:

To promote self-disclosure with others in order to improve communication skills and strengthen relationships.

To increase self-awareness and self-understanding.

II. GENERAL COMMENTS:

Acknowledging and understanding one's own values allows greater potential for self-disclosures and honest communication between individuals. Self-understanding has the potential to positively influence relationships.

III. POSSIBLE ACTIVITIES:

A. 1. Prepare activity by taking one handout and cutting ten strips of paper from the ten open-ended statements. Fold, and place in hat.

2. Generate discussion regarding self-disclosures, communication, and relationships.

3. Encourage each group member to choose a strip of paper from the hat, read aloud, and complete the self-disclosure statement. Place paper into hat when finished.

4. Continue with all group members for a designated time period.

5. As a closure, ask all group members to identify one significant person they plan to share their self-disclosures with, and how it might affect that relationship.

6. Process benefits of this activity.

B. 1. Distribute handouts, encouraging group members to complete the sentences, writing their responses on the lines provided.

2. Facilitate a discussion of each statement, encouraging individuals to share.

3. As a closure, ask all group members to identify one significant person they plan to share their self-disclosures with, and how it might affect that relationship.

4. Process benefits of this activity.

WOULDA SHOULDA COULDA

	What are some self-defeating statements that you make?	How can you *reframe* these as positive self-talk statements?
WOULDA		
SHOULDA		
COULDA		

WOULDA
SHOULDA
COULDA

I. PURPOSE:

To increase communication skills by developing an awareness of self-defeating statements.

To learn how to reframe self-defeating statements for increased personal strength and self-control.

II. GENERAL COMMENTS:

The "WOULDA... SHOULDA... COULDA" habit places unnecessary pressures on an individual. These statements are often made after an event has taken place and the situation cannot be changed. Rather than blaming oneself over a past event, new healthier ways can be identified to perceive the situation. "Reframing" allows the same subject to be viewed differently — the "old frame" is self-defeating, and the "new frame" enhances self-esteem. It is helpful to remind group members that a person does the best s/he can, given the awareness s/he has at *that* time.

III. POSSIBLE ACTIVITIES:

A. 1. Distribute handouts.

2. Discuss the "WOULDA... SHOULDA... COULDA" habit and its effects on an individual's self-esteem and stress level.

3. Ask for examples of the various self-defeating statements, demonstrating possible ways to reframe.

4. Instruct all group members to complete handout by writing 3 different examples from their personal lives.

5. Ask each group member to read one statement from each category, giving first the self-defeating version, and second, the reframed version.

6. Process benefits of this activity.

B. 1. Introduce topic.

2. Explain further by using examples from the group or these examples:

SELF-DEFEATING STATEMENTS	POSITIVE SELF-TALK STATEMENTS
(Educational)	
I "shoulda" stayed in school longer and finished high school.	I needed those wild years back then, to become the determined person I am today. I'll get my G.E.D.
(Professional, financial, personal)	
I "woulda" been able to work and make money if I didn't have the baby.	I'll be able to work for years to come. My most important job now, is to be home and raise a family.
(Personal/financial)	
I "coulda" bought a nicer home if my folks would've helped with the down payment.	I am proud of what we have and for not overextending our budget.

3. Distribute handouts encouraging group members to complete. Ask group members to choose one area where they use self-defeating statements most often: professional, personal, financial, social and educational.

4. Facilitate discussion of volunteered responses.

5. Process benefits of this activity.

COMMUNICATION
BUILDING BLOCKS

1

6

11

2

7

12

3

8

13

4

9

14

5

10

15

COMMUNICATION
BUILDING BLOCKS

I. PURPOSE:

To increase an awareness of verbal, nonverbal, one-way and two-way communication.

To promote open communication.

II. GENERAL COMMENTS:

Open communication which involves verbal, nonverbal, and two-way communication offers the clearest *picture* to the receiver. Effective communication promotes improved personal and professional relationships.

III. POSSIBLE ACTIVITIES:

A. 1. Photocopy 1 handout.

2. Distribute blank paper and pencils to all group members.

3. Ask for a volunteer, and instruct him/her (without showing the handout to others) to...
    a. choose one shape.
    b. describe it to the group using verbal cues only, so the others can accurately draw it on their papers. Use one-way communication only. Do not allow questions/comments from the group. Do not use nonverbal cues (hand motions, body gestures, etc.).

4. Encourage group members to show their drawings to the describer to compare their copies with the original.

5. Continue the activity by instructing volunteer #2 to describe a different shape verbally, but this time including nonverbal cues as well. Use one-way communication only.

6. Encourage group members to draw, and then show their drawings to the describer to compare their copies with the original.

7. Continue the activity by instructing volunteer #3 to describe a third shape verbally and nonverbally, allowing for two-way communication with group members.

8. Process the group by discussing members' reactions and responses to each of the 3 exercises, emphasizing the benefits of verbal, nonverbal and two-way communication.

B. 1. Photocopy one page and make cards of each of the twelve designs.

2. Encourage group members to describe their shapes to the rest of the group. They can choose to describe them... (a) verbally, with no nonverbal cues; (b) verbally and nonverbally, allowing no questions; or (c) verbally and nonverbally, encouraging questions.

3. Process the group by discussing members' reactions to the exercise, and emphasizing the benefits of open communication.

YOUR BODY CAN SPEAK

Your body has a language of its own.
Take a look at your body and the message you're sending to others.

Your Eyes

Attempt to be at eye level when communicating with others. Remember, maintaining good eye contact is important. Be aware of eyebrow gestures.

_____
_____
_____

Attempt to keep all facial muscles relaxed. Avoid tightening your jaw, clenching your teeth, and fidgety movements. It is recommended that the facial expression reflect the feeling you wish to communicate.

_____
_____

Your Facial

Expression

Your Shoulders

and Arms

Attempt to keep shoulders straight and back, arms relaxed and uncrossed. Avoid overuse of shoulder shrugging.

_____
_____
_____

Attempt to keep handshakes firm and decisive. Remember... not too long, not too short, not too rough, not too flimsy!!

_____
_____
_____

Your

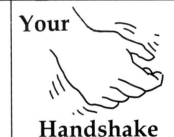

Handshake

Your Total Body

Gestures

Attempt soft, smooth motions, instead of quick, abrupt ones. Be aware of personal comfort zones and maintain adequate distances. Turn your entire body, and "face" the person you're communicating with directly.

_____
_____
_____
_____
_____
_____

YOUR BODY CAN SPEAK

I. PURPOSE:

To increase effective communication skills by recognizing and improving nonverbal messages.

II. GENERAL COMMENTS:

Communication is a vital key to meaningful and successful interactions and relationships. Nonverbal communication can be extremely powerful in setting the stage for effective communication.

III. POSSIBLE ACTIVITIES:

A. 1. Distribute handouts.

2. Discuss the potential for positive and negative messages to be sent nonverbally.

3. Set up didactic role-plays using the following situations, demonstrating both positive and negative messages:
   a) Ask spouse/teacher/friend for time to talk.
   b) Discuss possibilities of raise with boss/increased allowance with parents/more money for leisure-spending with spouse.
   c) Confer with teacher/professor about low grade.

4. Elicit feedback from group members after each role-play. Ask members to describe specific physical messages sent and how this affected the role-play.

5. Process benefits of recognizing and improving nonverbal messages.

B. 1. Discuss concept of body language.

2. Brainstorm on chalkboard the body language which accompanies assertive, passive, and aggressive communication, respectively.

3. Divide group into pairs.

4. Instruct group members to do mini-interviews with their partners. Each group member is to first attempt assertive body language during the interview and then accept feedback from his/her partner. Instruct group members to follow this format:
   a) exchange names.
   b) complete this sentence, "One thing I'm looking forward to is _____."
   c) discuss two pieces of personal information (background, family, age, education, etc.).
   d) give a handshake.

5. Reconvene as large group. Encourage group members to introduce their partners to the group.

6. Encourage feedback from the group about the introductions.

7. Process benefits of recognizing and improving nonverbal messages.

Depressed ? ?

Feeling Blue ? ? ? ?

What Can I Do ? ? ? ? ? ?

Which do you imagine yourself doing when you need to cope?

ASSERTING MYSELF	or	CONTACTING ONE OF MY SUPPORTS
CHANGING A HABIT	or	HELPING SOMEONE
GOING SHOPPING	or	LISTENING TO FAVORITE MUSIC
EATING SOMETHING HEALTHY	or	EXERCISING
TAKING A TRIP	or	TAKING A BREAK
LEARNING SOMETHING NEW	or	GOING TO A MOVIE
WRITING A LETTER OR IN A JOURNAL	or	READING A BOOK/MAGAZINE
TAKING A WALK	or	TALKING TO A FRIEND
TAKING A HOT BATH/SHOWER	or	LAUGHING/CRYING

Recognizing the importance of these valuable tools is the first step in establishing coping skills. The next step is exercising these skills when feeling depressed, to increase your sense of well-being!

Depressed ? ?

Feeling Blue ? ? ? ?

What Can I Do ? ? ? ? ? ?

I. PURPOSE:

To develop effective coping skills by identifying specific strategies to cope when feeling depressed.

II. GENERAL COMMENTS:

When feeling depressed, there is an overwhelming sense of sadness that often inhibits development and/or implementation of coping skills. It takes effort, motivation and/or support to identify specific strategies to cope, but they offer a sense of control and optimism for the future.

III. POSSIBLE ACTIVITIES:

A. 1. Provide a brief explanation of the benefits of developing individual coping skills.

2. Distribute handouts and instruct group members to choose one from each pair and complete by writing as many ideas as they have.
   For example:
   Asserting myself: "Sharing my feeling of loneliness with best friends."

   Changing a habit: "I'll only watch 2 hours of TV rather than my usual four or more."

3. Encourage group members to self-disclose as able.

4. Process benefits of having a plan of specific strategies to cope when feeling depressed.

B. 1. Provide a brief explanation of the benefits of developing individual coping skills.

2. Photocopy handout twice and cut into 36 cards.

3. Place cards in center of table. Ask a volunteer to choose a card and describe to the group how s/he might use that coping skill. Group members can *pass* on one card if they are unable to answer, and give it to the person on the right. They must choose the next card, however, and answer it.

4. Process benefits of having a plan of specific strategies to cope when feeling depressed.

LIMITS

1

2

3

4

By setting these limits, I am taking
more control of my life, increasing
my self-esteem, and establishing
boundaries in my relationships.

Signature:

_____

LIMITS

I. PURPOSE:

   To increase coping skills by identifying benefits of setting limits.

II. GENERAL COMMENTS:

   Limit setting establishes necessary personal boundaries. Vague limits often produce stress and anxiety. The ability to set limits is effective with oneself, and with others, in every area of life. The benefits of setting limits include increased sense of control, increased self-esteem and stress management, and improved quality of relationships... just to name a few!

III. POSSIBLE ACTIVITIES:

   A. 1. Distribute handouts, discussing topics and benefits.

       2. Ask group members to set two limits from each category:
          a) relationships with...
             1. parents   5. spouse/boyfriend/girlfriend
             2. children/siblings   6. boss/teacher
             3. neighbors   7. self
             4. friends   8. strangers

          b) activities related to...
             1. work   5. leisure
             2. home   6. self
             3. finances   7. religious affiliations
             4. education   8. community

       3. Remind group members to be as specific as possible, e.g., rephrase limits such as: "I will not get *stepped on* by my mother-in-law", to "I will limit my phone calls with my mother-in-law to one time per week".

       4. Encourage group members to share as able.

       5. Process how limit setting is an effective coping skill.

   B. 1. Distribute handouts, discussing topic and benefits.

       2. Brainstorm all possible relationships and activities which may need limit setting (see examples in A.2.).

       3. Instruct group members to write 4 limits on their handouts.

       4. Ask group members to role-play or state goals related to their identified limits.

       5. Encourage group members to share as able.

       6. Process how limit setting is an effective coping skill.

LOOK FOR ALTERNATIVES
WHEN ROADBLOCKED!

IN A "STEW"?
① Identify your problem.
② Identify your roadblock.
③ Look for alternatives!

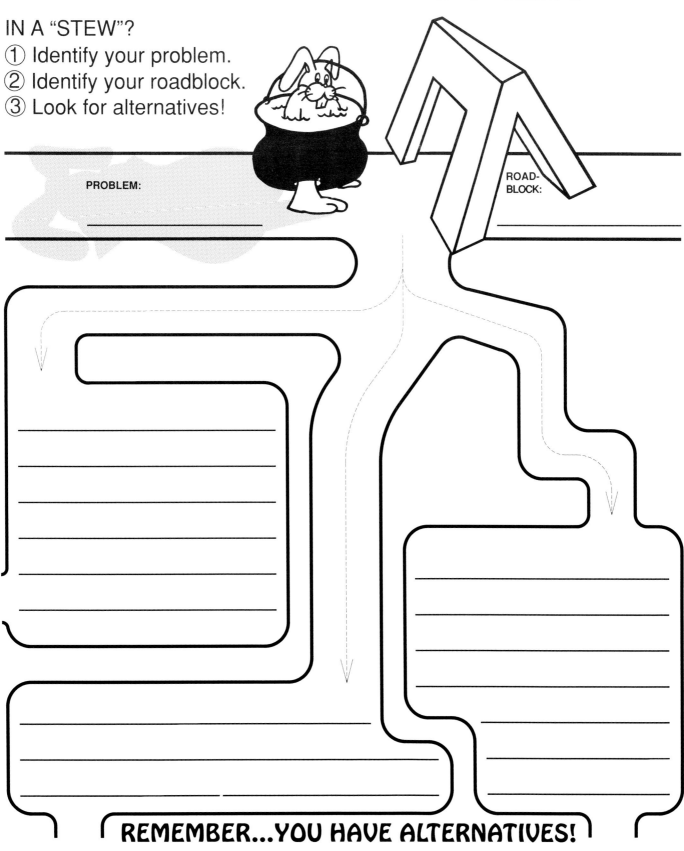

PROBLEM:
_____

ROAD-
BLOCK:
_____

REMEMBER...YOU HAVE ALTERNATIVES!

LOOK FOR ALTERNATIVES

I. PURPOSE:

To improve coping skills by recognizing potential roadblocks and by identifying possible options.

II. GENERAL COMMENTS:

When inundated by problems, it is easy to lose perspective and not see what the roadblocks are, or what the alternative choices might be. Identifying options is one effective coping skill.

III. POSSIBLE ACTIVITIES:

A. 1. Offer the following example or try to elicit one from the group:
   PROBLEM......My bills are overwhelming.
   ROADBLOCK..I use my credit cards excessively.

   ALTERNATIVES:

I'll give my credit cards back to the bank or cut them up.	I'll go to a consumer credit counseling service.	I'll get some sound advice about budgeting from my brother-in-law.

2. Distribute handouts and encourage group members to complete the handouts individually.

3. Facilitate discussion of individual's options, encouraging group members to offer feedback.

4. Discuss benefits of this skill.

B. 1. Distribute handout and ask each person to write a problem, at the top of the page, which s/he is experiencing.

2. Pass them to the right, or mix them up and pass them around, and ask each person to read the problem and identify possible options.

3. Return papers to original owners and ask if any of the solutions seem feasible to them.

4. Process benefits of looking at options and receiving ideas from others when facing a difficult problem.

M O T T O

GAME

I can cope, picturing these Wellness Mottos.

"HASTE MAKETH WASTE."	"A watched pot never boils."	*"Time flies when you're having fun."*	"An apple a day keeps the doctor away."	"Busy hands are happy hands."
"One day at a time."	"All work and no play makes Jack a dull boy."	"Just say NO."	"DON'T BURN THE CANDLE AT BOTH ENDS."	"Never put off til tomorrow what you can do today."
"Don't count your chickens before they hatch."	"Live and learn."	"STICKS AND STONES MAY BREAK MY BONES BUT NAMES WILL NEVER HURT ME."	*"That's what friends are for."*	"All for one and one for all."
"Better late than never."	"THE BEST THINGS IN LIFE ARE FREE."	"No one is an island."	"Don't cry over spilt milk."	"To err is human. To forgive divine."
"A friend in need is a friend indeed."	*"You're never too old to learn."*	*"A penny saved is a penny earned."*	"Procrastination is the thief of time."	*"Two heads are better than one."*
"You can't unscramble eggs."	"MANY HANDS MAKE LIGHT WORK."	"Take time to smell the roses."	"EARLY TO BED, EARLY TO RISE..."	"Don't sweat the small stuff."
"IF IT WORKS, DON'T FIX IT."	*"Look before you leap."*	"Honesty is the best policy."	"First things first."	*"To thine own self be true."*

M O T T O

I. PURPOSE:

To increase coping skills by adopting Wellness Mottos as personal mottos.

II. GENERAL COMMENTS

It is easy to overlook the wisdom that lies within these mottos. Reminiscing, discussing, thinking, and laughing assist in the integration of these thought-provoking mottos.

III. POSSIBLE ACTIVITIES:

A. 1. Photocopy one handout and cut into 35 cards.

2. Divide group into 2 teams, A & B.

3. Instruct one member from team A to choose a card and draw the motto on a chalkboard in front of his team. S/he is to draw pictures only, with no verbal cues to his team members, within a certain time limit (2 minutes). Award a correct response by giving 1 point. If team A is unable to give the correct response, offer team B thirty seconds to guess, and award them 1 point if correct.

4. List possible Wellness Topics:
   Assertiveness
   Leisure
   Life Balance
   Money Management
   Nutrition
   Self-Esteem
   Sleep
   Stress Management
   Support Systems
   Time Management
   Values

Instruct team with correct response to choose which Wellness Topic the motto fits into, and give one bonus point per "correct" guess.

5. Proceed with turn-taking between teams.

6. Play *lightning round* by instructing each team to choose one member to draw the clues. Allow 4 minutes for team A to guess as many mottos as possible. Proceed with team B.

7. At the end of each round, the other team may guess any unguessed mottos and receive the point.

8. Process favorite/meaningful mottos, encouraging group members to adopt mottos to assist them with coping.

B. 1. Revise "Motto Game" into "Motto Bingo" cards by covering 2 horizontal rows, leaving twenty-five mottos (5 across and 5 down), and photocopy as many as needed.

2. Distribute cards.

3. Play "Motto Bingo".

4. Process by asking group members to choose their favorite motto and explain how it assists them with coping.

Grief grabs you
when you're least prepared!

Do you:

- ☐ start to say something and forget what it was you wanted to say?
- ☐ feel lonely even though you are in a room filled with people?
- ☐ feel overwhelmed with the flooding of many emotions?
- ☐ forget what you were about to do 5 minutes ago?
- ☐ become upset when watching TV or a movie; when reading a newspaper or a book?
- ☐ try to go to sleep and see "replays"?
- ☐ have a difficult time concentrating?
- ☐ have a sense of being incomplete?
- ☐ misplace your keys constantly?
- ☐ cry for no apparent reason?
- ☐ feel cheated?
- ☐ feel a *twang* when you see a striking resemblance, a familiar hairdo, certain clothing?
- ☐ feel like staying in bed, or better yet, climbing under the bed?
- ☐ find it hard to imagine that others' lives go on? people are still laughing? the sun still shines?
- ☐ feel a sense of loss at Thanksgiving, Father or Mother's Day, other holidays?
- ☐ feel someone's missing even though you are surrounded by loved ones?
- ☐ wish your loved one, who is no longer in your life, could see your children, see what you are accomplishing, etc.?
- ☐ feel a tremendous sense of emptiness, void, or hole in your life?
- ☐ feel "shook-up" when you see a photograph unexpectedly?
- ☐ feel fine for a period of time, and get depressed again for no apparent reason?
- ☐ feel angry at your loved one whom you've lost, yourself, your family, or people who are trying to help you?
- ☐ feel as if your sense of values has changed — things that used to be important to you aren't important anymore?
- ☐ feel as if you should look different to others, and are surprised that they can't see your pain?
- ☐ other _____

feel saddened when:

- ☐ you smell a familiar cologne, shaving cream, etc.?
- ☐ you go to a religious ceremony? meaningful event?
- ☐ it's the anniversary date of a birthday? wedding? death? divorce?
- ☐ you go to a certain restaurant? certain place? certain neighborhood?
- ☐ you see the beauty of everything coming alive in spring? the leaves turning color in fall?
- ☐ you see a couple arm-in-arm?
- ☐ you see a father and son, mother and daughter, siblings, best friends, etc. together?
- ☐ you hear a certain song? certain type of music?
- ☐ other _____

. . . it'll get better . . . and if not better, it'll get different!

I. PURPOSE:

To facilitate the grief process by:
1) acknowledging often unrecognized symptoms and feelings, and
2) recognizing benefits of discussing grief in a group setting.

II. GENERAL COMMENTS:

Grief is an intense feeling of deep sorrow and sadness caused by a loss. Oftentimes when people are experiencing grief symptoms, they are feeling alone, isolated, and unsupported. It is important for people who are grieving to realize that they are not alone and that there are common grief symptoms and feelings.

III. POSSIBLE ACTIVITIES:

A. 1. Present concept of grief "grabbing" a person when s/he least expects it.

2. Ask group members to complete handouts by identifying which situations happen to them.

3. Discuss each situation, asking members to volunteer to share their experiences.

4. Pursue *other* comments, asking members to share what they wrote.

5. Discuss last thought on the bottom of the page, ". . . it'll get better . . . and if not better, it'll get different", and ask members if they've noticed a difference as time has passed.

6. Process the benefits of recognizing grief symptoms and feelings, and discussing grief in a group setting.

B. 1. Present concept of grief "grabbing" a person when s/he least expects it.

2. Ask group members to complete handouts by identifying which situations happen to them.

3. Discuss each situation, asking a member to volunteer to share an emotion that co-exists with grief in that particular situation. Assist group members by using a list of varied emotions. (See page 7 in *Life Management Skills*, book 1, or *Emotions* poster — refer to order form on back page).

4. Process the benefits of recognizing grief symptoms and feelings, and discussing grief in a group setting.

INSIDE OUTSIDE

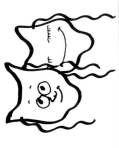

Name a situation in which you experience grief.	"Inside, I feel…" (*only I know that I am feeling…*)	"Outside, I appear…" (*other people view me as…*)	Implications of inside/outside discrepancy.
_____ _____ _____ _____ _____ _____ _____ _____ _____ _____	☐ aggressive ☐ alienated ☐ angry ☐ annoyed ☐ anxious ☐ apathetic ☐ bored ☐ cautious ☐ confident ☐ confused ☐ depressed ☐ determined ☐ disappointed ☐ discouraged ☐ disgusted ☐ embarrassed ☐ envious ☐ exhausted ☐ fearful ☐ frustrated ☐ guilty ☐ happy ☐ helpless ☐ hopeful ☐ hostile ☐ humiliated ☐ hurt ☐ hysterical ☐ innocent ☐ jealous ☐ lonely ☐ loved ☐ miserable ☐ negative ☐ optimistic ☐ pained ☐ paranoid ☐ peaceful ☐ puzzled ☐ regretful ☐ relieved ☐ sad ☐ shocked ☐ shy ☐ sorry ☐ stubborn ☐ surprised ☐ suspicious ☐ thoughtful ☐ undecided ☐ withdrawn ☐ _____	☐ aggressive ☐ alienated ☐ angry ☐ annoyed ☐ anxious ☐ apathetic ☐ bored ☐ cautious ☐ confident ☐ confused ☐ depressed ☐ determined ☐ disappointed ☐ discouraged ☐ disgusted ☐ embarrassed ☐ envious ☐ exhausted ☐ fearful ☐ frustrated ☐ guilty ☐ happy ☐ helpless ☐ hopeful ☐ hostile ☐ humiliated ☐ hurt ☐ hysterical ☐ innocent ☐ jealous ☐ lonely ☐ loved ☐ miserable ☐ negative ☐ optimistic ☐ pained ☐ paranoid ☐ peaceful ☐ puzzled ☐ regretful ☐ relieved ☐ sad ☐ shocked ☐ shy ☐ sorry ☐ stubborn ☐ surprised ☐ suspicious ☐ thoughtful ☐ undecided ☐ withdrawn ☐ _____	☐ Physical symptoms: _____ _____ _____ _____ ☐ Behavioral symptoms: _____ _____ _____ ☐ Emotional symptoms: _____ _____ _____

While it *is* OK to have some discrepancies between our feelings and expressions, it is also important to recognize that the greater this discrepancy, the greater the internal stress level. Bridging the gap between inside and outside can be done in several ways. What are some of your ideas?

INSIDE OUTSIDE

I. PURPOSE:

To gain insight regarding the discrepancy between how one feels and what one expresses while experiencing grief.

To identify 1) the physical, behavioral, and emotional implications of the "Inside, I Feel..."/ "Outside, I Appear..." discrepancy, and 2) ways to bridge the gap of this discrepancy.

II. GENERAL COMMENTS:

Oftentimes, people in grief feel that no one understands them. They often don't understand themselves. It might be due to discrepancies between emotion identification and emotion expression. It is vital to remind people that the greater the discrepancy, the greater the internal stress level. Further implications might involve...

    a) headaches, stomach problems, anxiety attacks.
    b) other people, due to reactions related to feelings from grief.
    c) confusion, frustration and/or ambivalence.

III. POSSIBLE ACTIVITIES:

A. 1. Explain concept of "Inside, I Feel..."/"Outside, I Appear..." using the following example:

Name a situation	Inside	Outside	Implications
anniversary of a loved one's death	[X] painful [X] confused [X] miserable [X] angry [X] annoyed [X] irritable	[X] hopeful [X] peaceful [X] determined [X] confident	physical: ulcer behavioral: relationship difficulties emotional: feel alone and unsupported

    2. Distribute handouts, instructing group members to complete.

    3. Ask group members to share, with emphasis on implications and ways to bridge the gap of this discrepancy.

    4. Process the activity.

B. 1. Explain concept of "Inside, I Feel..."/"Outside, I Appear..." using the following example:

Name a situation	Inside	Outside	Implications

loss of function	[X] angry
	[X] depressed
	[X] fearful
	[X] helpless
	[X] hostile
	[X] shocked
		[X] determined
		[X] hopeful
		[X] optimistic
			physical: migraine headaches
			behavioral: decreased productivity
			    at work
			emotional: feel confused, exhausted,
			    resentful that others aren't more
			    sensitive to my needs

    2. Distribute handouts, instructing group members to complete.

    3. Facilitate role-plays, by encouraging group members to choose situations in which they were unable to express their grief well.

    For example: It was the anniversary of a loved one's death and I was at work. I became angry when my boss asked me to do something, so I started an argument with my co-worker.

    4. Encourage group members to first do the role-play as the situation actually happened, and then work on communicating their grief more effectively.

    5. Ask group members to provide support and feedback for those who are role-playing.

    6. Process benefits of this activity.

TRY *IMAGERY* ...it can help!

Grief and losses can create stress and anxiety.

Are you experiencing any of the following losses?

Loss of a loved one? ☐   ☐ Loss of identity?
Loss of finances? ☐   ☐ Loss of childhood?
Loss of a home? ☐   ☐ Loss of lifestyle?
Loss of a pet? ☐   ☐ Loss of a job?
Loss of integrity? ☐   ☐ Loss of a project?
Loss of function? ☐   ☐ Loss of friend(s)?
_____ ☐   ☐ _____

If you've checked one or more of the above, you are FEELING a sense of loss —
in other words, you are grieving! You are entitled to grieve...
yet, grief is stressful and anxiety-provoking, creating problems both physically and emotionally.
One way to alleviate stress and anxiety is to take some time each day for yourself —
to relax, to nurture, and to heal.

Meditation and imagery can quiet your thoughts and settle your mind. To assist in this,
visualize an image that is soothing to you. Try to capture that image in the box below.

Use this image to nurture yourself.

I. PURPOSE:

To increase awareness of personal losses and grief and their effects.

To introduce the topic of imagery and relaxation to assist in grief work.

II. GENERAL COMMENTS:

It is common to underestimate the impact of a loss or multiple losses. It is important to recognize this stress and learn to cope, in an effort to maintain a sense of wellness. One helpful way to cope is with imagery and relaxation.

III. POSSIBLE ACTIVITIES:

A. 1. Distribute handouts, pens and colored markers. Introduce topic of imagery.

2. Encourage group members to complete handouts.

3. Share as able.

4. Listen to a relaxation tape, encouraging group members to visualize their *image*.

5. Process benefits of imagery and relaxation with grief and loss.

B. 1. Distribute blank paper, pens and colored markers to group members.

2. Introduce topic of imagery and relaxation to assist in grief work.

3. To assist in the creative process, ask group members to close their eyes and think of an image they associate with the word "soft".

4. Encourage group members to open their eyes and then draw or symbolize their image on their papers.

5. Continue process by using the words "quiet", "soothing", "relaxing", and "nurturing" to elicit different images, instructing group members to draw or symbolize these four additional images.

6. Ask group members to choose their favorite image and share it with the group.

7. Distribute handouts and encourage group members to complete.

8. Listen to a relaxation tape, encouraging group members to visualize their *image*.

9. Process benefits of imagery and relaxation with grief and loss.

Humor can help reduce stress. A lighter side *does* exist within most life situations. Our attitude, during even the more emotionally-packed events in our lives, can change our perspective *and* our ability to cope. Humor and laughter assist our physical and mental health. They elicit a natural healing response from our body; endorphins are released, which elevate mood, decrease pain sensation/perception, and make clearer reasoning possible.

The *Sunny-Side Up* approach does not make fun of situations, but encourages coping.

List below three emotionally-packed situations you're facing now or have experienced during the past year. Take a step back, and look at each situation from a lighter side... identifying a way in which you could see the situation (or part of it!) in a humorous way. Next, identify a humorous response to better cope with the situation.

	Emotionally-Packed Situation	Lighter Side Thought	Humorous Response/Action
M I L D	Bees attacked my picnic.	Even bees need to eat. Our food is <u>so</u> good, even the bees like it.	We left some drink and food out, and then moved away with the rest of our food and watched the bees for entertainment.
M O D E R A T E	I might be losing my job.	Then I'd have more time to be with my family and more time to spend on those exciting household repairs!	I'll have a resumé writing contest among my friends to see who can write the best resumé for me!
E X T R E M E	I'm grieving the loss of a good friend.	My friend always laughed in the strangest situations... and would probably be laughing now if he saw the dark circles under my eyes!	I'll pay tribute to my friend by reminiscing with old pictures of us having a good time together. I'll keep a log of strange situations I see that would make him laugh!

Try the *Sunny-Side Up* approach... to keep your life *unscrambled!*

Funny - Side Up

I. PURPOSE:

To increase coping skills through the use of humor with various life situations.

II. GENERAL COMMENTS:

Humor and laughter can be used as coping mechanisms with even the more emotionally-packed situations in life. Learning how to see a lighter side to various life situations and to find a humorous response/action, can contribute to improved physical and mental health.

III. POSSIBLE ACTIVITIES:

A. 1. Distribute handouts, and discuss humor as a coping skill.

2. Instruct group members to complete handouts.

3. Ask group members to share at least one of their three situations.

4. Encourage others to offer alternative lighter side thoughts and humorous responses/actions as feedback.

5. Process benefits of this activity.

B. 1. Introduce concept of humor as a method of coping with emotionally-packed situations.

2. Write the following situations on the chalkboard or develop a list of your own...
   a) I broke a dozen eggs on the floor.
   b) My mother never calls.
   c) There's no money to pay the bills.
   d) I broke my leg.
   e) My best friend is moving to another city.
   f) My flowers didn't arrive on time on my wedding day.
   g) I drove on a back road at 2:00 a.m. and my car broke down.
   h) It's very hot at a graduation ceremony.
   i) A relative unexpectedly needs to leave town.

3. Brainstorm lighter side thoughts and humorous responses/actions for each situation, and write on chalkboard.

4. Distribute handouts instructing group members to complete.

5. Share as able.

6. Process benefits of this activity.

Write in your own "Funnybone Ticklers" which can be integrated into your lifestyle for a healthier you!

Humor lets us feel more carefree and playful...what do you do that helps put you in a childlike/whimsical frame of mind?

_____

When we laugh with others, we share a special bond; as a group we are drawn together... recall your favorite memory of laughter with friends, family, co-workers, acquaintances.

_____

Being able to laugh at ourselves is a sign of healthy self-esteem... describe a time that you faced your own imperfections with laughter.

_____

Brightening up another person's day with humor brings many rewards... relate when you last made someone else laugh and you both felt great as a result!

_____

Although joke-telling is only one way to tickle your funnybone, many people enjoy jokes as a form of humor... can you remember a specific joke which made you laugh, recently or in the past? Why did that particular joke seem funny to you?

_____

The entertainment world is often a resource for humor... identify movies, shows, plays, or television programs that appeal to your sense of humor. Do you have a favorite comedian? Who?

_____

Children can teach us a lot about "letting go"... when did you last spend time laughing with little ones?

_____

Positive reactions to humor can be great stress and tension reducers... can you recall where you were and what happened when you last enjoyed a good belly laugh or uncontrollable laughter?

_____

"Humor is a prescription for good health" is a message with much value for our sense of well-being... describe one way that you can tap your sense of humor when you're not feeling your best.

_____

_There are certain things that happen and seem to _always_ make us laugh (or at least smile!)_... what is one thing that tickles your funnybone, time and time again?

_____

CONGRATULATIONS!!!
You can now pat yourself on the nose (others might say - your _back_), for a job well done!
You've successfully completed the membership application for the
"Humor-and-Health Club", and you're now an Honorary Funnybone Member!

I. PURPOSE:

To identify the many facets that characterize one's own sense of humor.

To recognize the value of humor as a coping skill.

II. GENERAL COMMENTS:

Oftentimes, we forget to tap our sense of humor to help us cope with day-to-day life. By first identifying *what* makes us laugh and *when*, we are one step closer to living a more *healthful* lifestyle.

III. POSSIBLE ACTIVITIES:

A. 1. Discuss concept of humor and related health benefits.

2. Distribute handouts and encourage group members to complete.

3. Encourage sharing of responses.

4. Process benefits of this activity, emphasizing individual differences in experience and expression of humor.

B. 1. Discuss concept of humor and related health benefits.

2. Photocopy one handout, cut into strips, and place in center of table.

3. Instruct first group member to choose one strip, read aloud, and respond. Then, ask all group members to complete the same question with their responses.

4. Proceed in clockwise direction until all strips are discussed.

5. Process by asking group members to...
    a) describe the role of humor in their lives, and its importance.
    b) identify ways they can increase humor in their lives.
    c) describe benefits of increasing humor.

SCHEDULE

NAME _____   Week of _____ / _____ / _____

	SUNDAY	MONDAY	TUESDAY	WEDNESDAY	THURSDAY	FRIDAY	SATURDAY
7:00							
8:00							
9:00							
10:00							
11:00							
12:00							
1:00							
2:00							
3:00							
4:00							
5:00							
6:00							
7:00							
8:00							
9:00							
10:00							

SCHEDULE

I. PURPOSE:

To identify daily activities for a one-week period in order to establish level of life balance or imbalance.

To acknowledge changes needed for improved life balance.

II. GENERAL COMMENTS:

Wellness can be defined in terms of an adequate life balance (leisure, individual care, free/unproductive time and efforts in work-activities). Identifying how time is spent on a weekly basis allows accurate analysis of strengths/weaknesses in one's scheduling.

III. POSSIBLE ACTIVITIES: This handout can be used in conjunction with BALANCE YOUR LIFE (page 27).

A. 1. Discuss concept of life balance and relationship to one's own stress level and self-concept.

2. Distribute 2 copies of handout per group member.

3. Instruct group members to choose a recent typical week and complete the schedule form according to how their time was spent (being as specific as possible).

4. Divide group into pairs for sharing of responses. Allow 15-20 minutes.

5. Reconvene as large group and encourage group members to share insights gained from the schedules and the discussions with partners.

6. Use second copy for follow-up activity or homework assignment. Instruct group members to complete the schedule form, as a proposed schedule, including needed changes and setting appropriate goals.

7. Process benefits of this activity.

B. 1. Use this handout for one-to-one sessions. Distribute the handouts as needed or include a schedule handout in admission packet.

2. Discuss concept of life balance and structure, in relationship to one's own stress level and self-concept.

3. Ask individuals to complete handout prior to discharge. Remind them to include adequate balance of leisure, individual care, free time and efforts in work-activities.

4. Encourage individuals to first share this possible schedule with a significant other(s) and then, with the facilitator.

5. Review schedule offering feedback as needed.

6. Process benefits of this activity.

WORK·LEISURE BALANCE

WORK   LEISURE

List 1, 2, or 3 of your WORK activities:

1) _____

2) _____

3) _____

List 1, 2, or 3 of your LEISURE activities:

1) _____

2) _____

3) _____

WORK ACTIVITIES			Check (✓) which activities satisfy your...	LEISURE ACTIVITIES		
1	2	3		1	2	3
			need to be with others?			
			need for intellectual stimulation?			
			need to be outdoors?			
			need to be respected?			
			need for a structured lifestyle?			
			need for money?			
			need for social life and/or friends and/or family?			
			need for laughter and/or play?			
			need for privacy and/or quiet?			
			need to express yourself?			
			need to maintain adequate physical health?			
			need to feel competent?			
			need to be creative and/or artistic?			
			need for independence?			

WORK·LEISURE BALANCE

I. PURPOSE:

To increase life balance by evaluating how present work and leisure activities are satisfying needs.

II. GENERAL COMMENTS:

Everyone has needs. It's important to have all needs met and ideally maintain a balance, so that work meets some and leisure meets others. This work-leisure balance promotes the concept that energy and time need to be distributed in more than one life area.

III. POSSIBLE ACTIVITIES:

A. 1. Distribute handouts and explain concept of work-leisure balance.

2. Instruct group members to complete.

3. Discuss and share.

4. Brainstorm ways to satisfy remaining needs that are unmet either by work or by leisure.

5. Process benefits of this activity.

B. 1. Distribute handouts and explain concept of work-leisure balance.

2. Instruct group members to complete.

3. Divide group into 2 subgroups.

4. Instruct one subgroup to problem-solve 2 WORK activities that would meet the first pair of needs on the handout,
   e.g., Need to be with others and need for intellectual stimulation might be...
       computer programming job, volunteering at the science lab.
   Instruct the subgroup to continue by identifying 2 WORK activities for each of the subsequent pairs.

5. The other subgroup will proceed with above activity, identifying 2 LEISURE activities for each of the 7 pairs of needs listed.

6. Reconvene as a large group, sharing activity ideas.

7. Conclude group by asking group members to identify one work or one leisure activity they might pursue as a result of this activity.

BALANCE
YOUR

LEISURE
INDIVIDUAL CARE
FREE/ UNPRODUCTIVE TIME
EFFORTS IN WORK-ACTIVITIES

Clock labels: 12:00 am, 1:00 am, 2:00 am, 3:00 am, 4:00 am, 5:00 am, 6:00 am, 7:00 am, 8:00 am, 9:00 am, 10:00 am, 11:00 am, 12:00 pm, 1:00 pm, 2:00 pm, 3:00 pm, 4:00 pm, 5:00 pm, 6:00 pm, 7:00 pm, 8:00 pm, 9:00 pm, 10:00 pm, 11:00 pm

I. PURPOSE:

To increase awareness of how much time is spent daily in the 4 life areas:
   leisure, individual care, free/unproductive time and efforts in work-activities.

To identify a plan which provides a healthy daily balance among these 4 life areas.

II. GENERAL COMMENTS:

Life balance contributes to a healthy self-concept and to an individual's ability to cope with stress. There is not a set amount of time that is recommended for each life area, however, individuals need to determine and control their own healthy balance of activities.

III. POSSIBLE ACTIVITIES: This handout can be used in conjunction with SCHEDULE (page 25).

A. 1. Discuss concept of life balance and relationship to one's own stress level and self-concept.

   2. Distribute 2 copies of handout to group members.

   3. Instruct group members to complete one copy depicting how their lives are now, and the other copy depicting how they would like it to be.

   4. Provide each group member with 4 colored pencils or markers, corresponding with the colors assigned to the 4 life areas, e.g.,

      Leisure . . . . Blue   Free/unproductive time . . . . . Red
      Individual care . . . . Green   Efforts in work-activities . . . . Yellow

   5. Instruct group members to color each section of their balance wheel with one of the 4 colors, depending on how they spend that hour of the day. All 24 hours will be colored in. The use of color will be a visual demonstration of balance/imbalance.

   6. Share responses as a group and assist members to analyze their balance wheels for areas of difficulty.

   7. Use second copy of handout for follow-up activity or homework assignment.

   8. Process benefits of this activity.

B. 1. Distribute handouts. Discuss concept of life balance and relationship to one's own stress level and self-concept.

   2. Encourage group members to complete the handout by writing in all of their specific daily activities, e.g., taking care of children, listening to music, bathing, etc.

   3. Ask group members to categorize these activities into life areas: leisure, individual care, free time and efforts in work-activities.

   4. Share responses as a group and assist members to analyze their balance wheels for areas of difficulty.

   5. Process benefits of this activity.

MONEY MANAGEMENT

(or the lack thereof)

Evaluate your spending habits by circling ⓐ or ⓑ:

1. **a.** I buy something when I feel like it.
   b. I buy things only after much consideration.

2. **a.** I seldom spend money on leisure or entertainment.
   b. I prioritize leisure and spend money on it.

3. **a.** I put money in savings.
   b. I scrounge money weekly with nothing left over for savings.

4. **a.** If I buy a major item, I go to a store and buy it, saving time by not comparing prices.
   b. If I buy a major item, I compare prices, read up on the best product, and then buy.

5. **a.** I plan credit card purchases and pay the full balance when it's due.
   b. I overextend on credit cards, paying only part of the full balance each month.

6. **a.** I can control cash in my hand / wallet, or I make sure I never have cash "on hand".
   b. Cash is a "trigger" for me to spend.

7. **a.** I never spend money on myself.
   b. I choose to spend some money on myself.

8. **a.** I confront my financial situation, evaluating and updating as time passes.
   b. My money has a mind of its own; I allow my money to run itself.

9. **a.** I manage my money independently — not asking for others' help.
   b. I ask for help from those who can manage money better than I.

10. **a.** I know my income, expenses and budget, and plan accordingly.
    b. I don't know my financial situation, so I don't plan.

 G⊕AL ***Which one of the above ten issues are you willing to address?***

_____

 G⊕AL ***How can you make changes in this area?***

_____

MONEY MANAGEMENT (or the lack thereof)

I. PURPOSE:

To increase awareness of personal spending habits.

To recognize areas of difficulty with money management.

II. GENERAL COMMENTS:

Several factors affect the ability to manage or mismanage money. Some include:

1.) impulsivity,
2.) leisure values,
3.) ability to plan,
4.) organizing and planning,
5.) values regarding credit,
6.) immediate vs. delayed gratification,
7.) self-esteem/self-image,
8.) tendencies to avoid/confront,
9.) ability to manage money independently,
10.) awareness of financial situation.

These areas can be evaluated to increase an individual's awareness. Implications for change need to be considered.

III. POSSIBLE ACTIVITIES:

A. 1. Distribute handouts.

2. Encourage each group member to complete.

3. Discuss each question #1 through #10 with above outline.

4. Assist group members in setting goals to change specific areas.

5. Process benefits of this activity.

B. 1. Photocopy handout and cut each question #1 through #10, a & b, into separate strips of paper (making 20 strips). Place all in basket.

2. Encourage each group member to take one strip from the basket and respond accordingly. Discuss as needed.

3. Assist group members in setting goals to change specific areas.

4. Process benefits of this activity.

BUDGET WORK$HEET

BEFORE

AFTER

+ Monthly Income(s)

Taxes / deductions taken out . . . . $ _____

\+ $ _____

TOTAL INCOME(S) $ _____

− Monthly Expenses

Housing expense: rent / mortgage . . . . $ _____

Utilities: gas . . . . $ _____

electricity . . . . $ _____

water / sewer . . . . $ _____

garbage . . . . $ _____

Telephone . . . . $ _____

Transportation expense: fares . . . . $ _____

car payment . . . . $ _____

gasoline . . . . $ _____

insurance . . . . $ _____

Insurance / health care . . . . $ _____

Food . . . . $ _____

Entertainment . . . . $ _____

Clothing . . . . $ _____

Credit card(s) . . . . $ _____

Loan(s) . . . . $ _____

Child-care / parent-care . . . . $ _____

Other(s) . . . . $ _____

\+ $ _____

TOTAL EXPENSES $ _____

TOTAL INCOME(S) − **TOTAL EXPENSES** = **AMOUNT LEFT OVER / UNDER**

$ _____ − $ _____ = $ _____

PROBLEM AREA(S):

G@ALS:

BUDGET WORK$HEET

I. PURPOSE:

To assess financial status.

To increase money management by identifying problem areas and setting financial goals.

II. GENERAL COMMENTS:

Ineffective money management can be a stressor. It is common to avoid confronting one's financial status to *protect* oneself from additional stress. However, a written review of one's financial situation can, in the long run, reduce stress and the possibility of mismanaging funds.

III. POSSIBLE ACTIVITIES:

A. 1. As a one-to-one activity, provide individual with the budget worksheet and complete it together.

2. Assess with the individual his/her financial status.

3. Discuss problem areas, and establish realistic goals.

4. Process benefits of this activity.

B. 1. Discuss money management as a potential stress factor.

2. Present *budget* concept as a means of gaining control over financial stress.

3. Brainstorm list of possible monthly expense categories (fixed and variable) from group members and write on chalkboard. Some examples of monthly expenses are: toys, gifts, pets, furniture, furnishings, yard, upkeep of home, alimony, vacation, and repairs. Brainstorm possible sources of income, e.g., gift of money, part-time work, interest income, sale of a belonging, etc.

4. Discuss possible options for increasing income or decreasing expenses.

5. Distribute handouts and instruct group members to complete.

6. Encourage group members to share their goals, and request feedback from others.

7. Process benefits of a written review of finances.

BUYING HAPPINE$$

?????????????????????????

**One ineffective coping skill is trying to "buy happiness". This is just temporary...
a "band-aid"... often leading to post-purchase guilts, depression, embarrassment,
dissatisfaction, stress, and perhaps, financial debt.**

Do you...

1. binge-buy? (clothes, shoes, "sale" items, groceries) . . . . yes ___ no ___

   the last time? _____

2. gamble excessively? (horse races, lottery tickets, card games, bingo) . . . . yes ___ no ___

   the last time? _____

3. buy status objects? (jewelry, cars, furniture, name-brand items) . . . . yes ___ no ___

   the last time? _____

4. buy impulsively? (clothing, gadgets, fad items) . . . . yes ___ no ___

   the last time? _____

5. spend excessively on others? (too expensive or too many gifts, excessively on charities) . . yes ___ no ___

   the last time? _____

6. spend to avoid unpleasant situations (vacation, traveling to get away from problems) . . . yes ___ no ___

   the last time? _____

When/why do you do the above? _____

_____

What are potential implications of these habits? _____

_____

The next time you feel the
urge to buy... take out this
wallet-size card and ask
yourself these questions
before you make the
purchase.

> ### BUYING HAPPINE$$????
>
> *Will I be pleased with my purchase
> tomorrow... next week...next month... etc?*
>
> *Am I able to afford this?*
>
> *Do I want to spend my money on this right now?*
>
> *Why am I REALLY buying this?*
>
> *Am I OK with my reason for making this purchase?*

BUYING HAPPINE$$????

I. PURPOSE:

To increase money management skills by:
1. recognizing self-defeating money management habits,
2. learning a self-questioning method to avoid these habits.

II. GENERAL COMMENTS:

Oftentimes when depressed, anxious or stressed, it is a first impulse to SPEND in order to
buy happiness. This "habit" or tendency is often self-defeating, leading to negative consequences.

III. POSSIBLE ACTIVITIES:

A. 1. Distribute handouts.

2. Explain interrelationship that money can have with emotional well-being.

3. Encourage group members to complete handout.

4. Review self-questioning method, discussing benefits.

5. Process benefits of this activity.

B. 1. Explain interrelationship that money can have with emotional well-being.

2. List on chalkboard the 6 following categories:
   binge-buying
   gambling excessively
   buying status objects
   buying impulsively/on a whim
   overspending on others
   spending to avoid unpleasant situations

3. Encourage group members to:
   a. self-disclose as able, personal tendencies in each category, and
   b. brainstorm list of whys and whens.

4. Distribute handouts.

5. Encourage group members to complete handout.

6. Review self-questioning method, discussing benefits.

7 Process benefits of this activity.

POSITIVE PARENTING SKILLS

One positive parenting skill is communication involving both listening and talking, in a mutually respectful manner. We communicate with our body language, our actions, and our words. The open communication style of listening with interest and understanding, and expressing our thoughts and feelings using "I" messages, will enhance relationships. Positive "You-seem" messages can be used effectively when you want to reflect the children's feelings back to them and/or clarify their feelings. Follow-up, open-ended questions allow for further communication.

At times, during emotionally-packed situations, we *may* resort to previous ineffective communication habits we were exposed to in the past. Negative "You" messages are ineffective for a number of reasons, including attaching a label to the child, closing the door on effective communication, blaming the child for our feelings, etc.

Now, your turn to practice...

	Situation	Negative "You" message (labeling, blaming, ridiculing, etc.)	"I" message (expressing our thoughts/feelings)	Positive "You-Seem" message (reflecting back and/or clarifying child's feelings) with Follow-up, open-ended question
E X A M P L E S	Your 10 year-old child is getting low grades at school.	*You can't do anything right! You're a poor student!*	*I'm concerned about your grades.*	*You seem disinterested in your school work lately with low grades this last report card. What's going on?*
	Your 4 year-old child begins to act-out at a restaurant.	*You're so bad at restaurants, we can't take you anywhere!*	*I'm disappointed when you act-out. I want to be able to bring you with us when we go out to eat.*	*You seem bored with sitting here. Is there something you can do to be more relaxed/comfortable?*
	You suspect your teenager has been experimenting with drugs.	*You've been using drugs, I just know it! You won't amount to anything! You're no good!*	*I'm worried that you've been trying drugs and I don't want anything to happen to you. Let's talk about it.*	*You seem distant from us lately. It seems like you're getting pressure from your friends. What can I do to help?*
1.				
2.				
3.				

Establishing positive communication with your child today, will lay the foundation for your relationship in the future.

POSITIVE PARENTING SKILLS

I. PURPOSE:

To identify and practice positive communication skills to enhance parenting.

To recognize ineffective means of communicating with children.

II. GENERAL COMMENTS:

A fundamental parenting skill is communication. Positive communication with children enhances relationships, establishing a sense of self-worth for both children and adults. Learning to use "I" messages, and positive "you-seem" messages (with follow-up, open-ended questions), increases communication skills.

III. POSSIBLE ACTIVITIES:

A. 1. Introduce concept of positive communication skills and benefits.

2. Distribute handouts and review, emphasizing need for practice in order to improve communication and enhance relationships.

3. Ask group members to complete handout.

4. Encourage group members to choose one situation and role-play, attempting to use positive communication skills.

5. Facilitate feedback and support from others.

6. Process benefits of this activity.

B. 1. Introduce concept of positive communication skills and benefits.

2. Define terms "I" messages, positive "you-seem" messages (with follow-up, open-ended questions), and negative "you" messages.

3. Use the following situations or your own:
   a) Your 3 year-old is having a temper tantrum in the department store.
   b) Your 7 year-old rides his/her bicycle in the street without permission.
   c) You catch your 10 year-old and 13 year-old playing with matches.
   d) Your 15 year-old comes home one hour late after curfew.
   e) Your 17 year-old has been unusually quiet lately.

Instruct group to brainstorm possible "I" messages, and "you-seem" messages (with follow-up, open-ended questions).

4. Distribute handouts, instructing each group member to complete with personal examples.

5. Ask group members to share.

6. Process benefits of positive communication with children.

Nurturing Self-Esteem in Children

YOU ARE IN A UNIQUE POSITION TO INFLUENCE CHILDREN'S SELF-ESTEEM!

Read the following and fill in the appropriate blanks to complete the self-esteem tips for children.
Use each word in the list below only once.

1. Use *two-way* communication *with* children, both _____ and _____, rather than *one-way* communication, or talking *at* children. Two-way communication shows respect for children, and reinforces that they are worthwhile and valuable.

2. Say more "_____," than "don'ts", e.g., "Hold the baby carefully" rather than "Don't hold the baby like that!" *or* "Please put your coat in the closet" rather than "Don't throw your coat on the floor!". "Do's" help children learn to be _____ and competent.

3. Communicate with children as you would with friends or other adults. The _____ you show children will strengthen your relationship. Use common _____ such as "please", "thank you", etc.

4. _____ children's _____ and help them to express them openly. Remember not to label feelings as good or bad; we *all* experience *all* feelings at one time or another. You can take an active role in helping children learn to express these feelings effectively.

5. Allow children to feel accepted, loved, and wanted, even though their behavior at times may not be O.K., e.g., as a father, you love your son — yet you do not accept his behavior when fighting with his classmates. Separate the _____ and worth of the child from his/her _____, e.g., "I'm concerned about your fighting at school; it needs to stop. You seem to be angry about something. How can I help?"

6. When _____ *your* feelings and thoughts to children, focus on _____, e.g., "I need you to clean up your room now before our company comes over" rather than "you messed up everything in here, and you knew we had company coming over at 6:00. You're such a slob!" Avoid messages that label and ridicule children.

7. Spend time _____ with children. A positive sense of humor is _____ for everyone!

8. Help children learn positive _____ skills so they feel _____ _____ with others in a variety of situations, e.g., "Hi, it's nice to meet you", "Hello... who's calling, please?","Thank you for the compliment ", "I'll share...".

9. Encourage participation in _____ activities, especially at an early age, so as not to place a lot of emphasis on "Who's the best?" or being better than someone else. With competitive activities, encourage _____ and feeling O.K. with performance (regardless of "winning" or "losing"). Allow children to feel O.K. about their "personal best", rather than being *better* than others.

10. Assist children with learning effective problem-solving and _____ skills through play-acting, role-playing, or talking through various _____ for different situations. Encourage children to solve their own problems and make their own decisions as much as possible.

11. _____ children by using words and/or phrases, such as: "Keep up the good work!", "I love you", "Great job!", and by giving _____, such as: "I like the way you shared with your friends at the playground today", "I'm impressed!", "You deserve it — you're worth it!", "I know you're working hard on your homework".

12. Show children that they can _____ you and that you can trust them. Be _____, open, and direct when communicating.

13. Offer activities with which children can be _____ so they can experience feeling competent and a sense of _____ .

14. _____ children to make mistakes. Help them to accept this as a _____ quality, and value the learning they gain from these mistakes.

15. Remember... children will learn more by *what you do than what you say*. Be a _____ by showing positive self-esteem and _____ in yourself!

WORD LIST

achievement	communicating	decision-making	healthy	listening	social
acknowledge	compliments	do's	honest	noncompetitive	successful
allow	confidence	encourage	human	options	talking
behavior	consideration	feelings	"I" messages	role-model	trust
comfortable	courtesies	fun	laughing	self-assured	value

I. PURPOSE:

To recognize parenting influences on children's self-esteem.

To identify ways to enhance children's self-esteem.

II. GENERAL COMMENTS:

Self-esteem is vital in developing day-to-day life skills. Those in the parenting role have a significant impact on the ongoing development of self-esteem in children.

III. POSSIBLE ACTIVITIES:

A. 1. Discuss parenting influences on children's self-esteem and life-skill development.

2. Brainstorm on chalkboard group members' ideas for nurturing children's self-esteem.

3. Elicit comments from group members regarding their own childhood experiences with self-esteem, their present attitudes about self-esteem, and how these experiences and attitudes influence their parenting styles.

4. Distribute handouts and review, noting which parenting tips were not on the group's list, and which ones need practice and attention from group members.

WORD LIST KEY

(1) talking listening	(6) communicating "I" messages	(11) encourage compliments
(2) do's self-assured	(7) laughing healthy	(12) trust honest
(3) consideration courtesies	(8) social comfortable	(13) successful achievement
(4) acknowledge feelings	(9) noncompetitive fun	(14) allow human
(5) value behavior	(10) decision-making options	(15) role-model confidence

5. Process benefits of this group.

B. 1. Discuss parenting influences on children's self-esteem and life-skill development.

2. Divide group into 2-3 subgroups.

3. Distribute handouts to group members, encouraging teamwork to complete handout.

4. Ask group members to write down a specific example and description of how they could implement or have implemented this tip with children,

e.g., (1.) When my 7 year-old comes home from school.

5. Reconvene as a large group.

6. Review handout to check for correct answers and share subgroups' examples.

7. Process benefits of this group.

SIGNIFICANT LIFE EVENTS

Event	Age	EMOTIONS

SIGNIFICANT LIFE EVENTS

I. PURPOSE:

To promote recall of positive and negative events which had a significant effect on one's life.

To increase self-awareness of emotions associated with significant life events.

II. GENERAL COMMENTS:

Taking an inventory of one's past can often increase insights regarding present attitudes and behaviors. By reminiscing or reviewing life events, one can evaluate past experiences, influences, and patterns. This can assist in determining future directions.

III. POSSIBLE ACTIVITIES:

A. 1. Introduce concept with the following examples or one of your own:

Event	Age	Emotions
divorce of my parents	7	anger, hurt, resentment, fear
married my spouse	23	love, hope, joy, excitement

* Note: emphasize that at times we have mixed emotions about an event; emotions are not always all positive or all negative as in these 2 examples.

2. Encourage each group member to complete the handout, depicting his/her own significant life events through words, pictures, symbols.

3. Instruct group members to find a partner, and allow approximately 10-15 minutes for an "interview".

4. Reconvene the group at the end of the "interview", and ask each person to describe his/her partner's significant life events.

5. Process the group by discussing insights gained from this activity.

B. 1. Introduce concept with the following examples or one of your own:

Event	Age	Emotions
divorce of my parents	7	anger, hurt, resentment, fear
married my spouse	23	love, hope, joy, excitement

* Note: emphasize that at times we have mixed emotions about an event; emotions are not always all positive or all negative as in these 2 examples.

2. Divide group into subgroups of 2 or 3. Distribute 1 handout to each subgroup. Encourage subgroup to choose a famous or meaningful character and complete the handout as if they were the character. Here are some ideas:
   a) Anne Frank
   b) Tom Sawyer
   c) Richard Nixon
   d) George Bush
   e) Sugar Ray Leonard

3. Regroup, encouraging a representative of each subgroup to share their findings.

4. Distribute handout and instruct each group member to complete his/her own.

5. Encourage group members to share as able.

6. Process benefits of this activity.

What did I want to be when I grew up?

WHAT DID I WANT TO BE WHEN I GREW UP?	WAS THIS REALISTIC?	IF YES — DID I ACCOMPLISH THIS? HOW? / WHY NOT?	IF NO — WHY WASN'T THIS REALISTIC?	HOW DO I FEEL ABOUT THIS?	IS THERE ANYTHING I DO OR COULD DO TODAY TO TOUCH THESE DREAMS?
	☐ Yes ☐ No				
	☐ Yes ☐ No				
	☐ Yes ☐ No				
	☐ Yes ☐ No				

*What
did
I want to be
when I grew up
?*

I. PURPOSE:

To reminisce about earlier hopes/dreams.

To increase awareness of emotions surrounding these hopes/dreams.

II. GENERAL COMMENTS:

All of us have had hopes for the future — some fulfilled and others not. It can be therapeutic to reflect on our hopes and hear others'. If unfulfilled, perhaps there is still room to "touch" these dreams.

III. POSSIBLE ACTIVITIES:

A. 1. Distribute handouts.

2. Explain using following example:

princess	☐ Y ☒ N	wasn't born in the "right" family	OK	read about Princess Di and Fergie, read fairy tales, encourage my children to play princesses

3. Encourage group members to complete handouts.

4. Collect handouts and read aloud, encouraging group members to guess the author of each.

5. Process benefits of this activity.

B. 1. Distribute handouts.

2. Explain using following example:

pro baseball player	☒ Y ☐ N	no, I had a knee injury	sad	go to the ball park and cheer for my favorite player; I coach a neighborhood softball league.

3. Encourage group members to complete handouts.

4. Divide group into two teams. Encourage group members from Team 1 to act out *wished* roles from their handouts for their own team members. Give 2 points to the team with the correct guess if no verbal clues were needed. Give 1 point with a correct guess if verbal clues were needed.

5. Encourage turn-taking between teams.

6. Process benefits of this activity.

your "first kiss"?	your first hospital visit/experience?	your first job or interview?
your first "best" friend?	a special place when you were a child?	where you were when a president died or a war broke out?
your first loss?	your favorite toy?	a favorite holiday tradition?
a favorite teacher?	your earliest scare?	an early memorable success?
your earliest disappointment?	your first circus/ carnival/ amusement park?	a town/city from your childhood?

Do you remember...   Do you remember...   Do you remember...

DO YOU REMEMBER...

I. PURPOSE:

To reminisce about significant ''firsts'' in a nonthreatening way.

To increase interaction with others by sharing personal life stories.

II. GENERAL COMMENTS:

Everyone has significant ''firsts''. Oftentimes, they were emotionally-packed... scary, exciting, upsetting, sad, funny. Sharing and listening to each other's life stories offers an interesting, fun, and therapeutic experience.

III. POSSIBLE ACTIVITIES:

A. 1. Distribute handouts.

2. Instruct group members to choose any two events and illustrate with pictures or symbols on the reverse side of the handout.

3. Collect handouts and ask group members to guess the artist of each. Encourage discussion.

4. Process benefits of this activity.

B. 1. Develop card game by cutting handout into 15 cards.

2. Place cards in center of table and instruct a group member to choose a card and share.

3. Continue until all group members have had an opportunity to share.

4. Process benefits of this activity.

ASSERTIVE RIGHTS

Include these *rights* in your everyday thinking and gain self-respect, as well as respect from others.

I have the right to . . .

1. _____ say "NO."
2. _____ be competent and proud of my accomplishments.
3. _____ feel and express anger.
4. _____ be treated as a capable human being.
5. _____ make mistakes and be responsible for them.
6. _____ change a situation.
7. _____ say "I don't know, I don't agree, and I don't understand."
8. _____ be treated with respect.
9. _____ express my needs, opinions, thoughts, ideas, and feelings.
10. _____ judge my own behavior and be responsible for it.
11. _____ take pride in my body and define attractiveness in my own terms.
12. _____ have a support system.
13. _____ be myself and have a separate identity.
14. _____ structure my own time priorities.
15. _____ request help and receive information from others.
16. _____ ask and not assume.
17. _____ have privacy.
18. _____ say "I'm not willing to accept that responsibility."
19. _____ be imperfect.
20. _____ grow, learn, change, and to value my age and experience.
21. _____ recognize MY needs as important.
22. _____ _____
23. _____ _____
24. _____ _____
25. _____ _____

ASSERTIVE RIGHTS

I. PURPOSE:

To increase assertive skills by recognizing assertive rights.

II. GENERAL COMMENTS:

Assertive rights are often overlooked. Many people were never taught these *rights* as children, and many are in relationships infringing on these *rights*. Recognizing and exercising these assertive rights empower people, offering a sense of control and dignity.

III. POSSIBLE ACTIVITIES:

A. 1. Distribute handouts

2. Encourage each group member to choose one *right* and explain it to the group, stating why it's important and ways to exercise that *right*

3. Consider as a follow-up activity, role-playing the "difficult" assertive rights and processing the benefits of exercising these *rights*

B. 1. Distribute handouts.

2. Discuss concept of assertive rights.

3. Instruct each group member to check off those *rights* that are difficult for him/her to accept and live by

4. Encourage each group member to stand and read aloud those statements he/she has checked, beginning with "I _____ have the *right* to _____."

5. Ask each group member to conclude with one goal.

6. Encourage applause for efforts after each member shares.

7. Process benefits of this activity.

SAFETY...
OUTSIDE THE HOME

How safe are you outside of your home??? Rate yourself:

0 = NEVER   1 = SOMETIMES   2 = ALWAYS

A ____ When leaving your home, do you put your extra house keys somewhere other than in a flowerpot or under a doormat?

B ____ When outside, do you look around?

C ____ Are you aware of safe spaces and safe distances?

D ____ Are you aware of high-risk and low-risk areas?

E ____ Would you be able to describe surroundings?

F ____ Are you ready to think, to move, or to scream/yell at a moment's notice?

G ____ Do you trust your instincts?

H ____ Do you leave a situation/place if you feel uncomfortable?

I ____ Are you careful of which people you talk to?

J ____ Are you careful of what you say when talking to strangers/acquaintances?

K ____ Do you carry keys in your hands?

L ____ Do you remember your body language, giving the appearance of being aware, alert and assertive?

M ____ Do you carry purse/wallet/money only if necessary?

N ____ Do you keep money and valuables close to body and conceal, if possible?

O ____ Do you wear your safety belt as a driver and as a passenger?

P ____ Do you keep car doors locked, even when stopped in an emergency?

Q ____ Do you keep an index card in your car with phone numbers of significant others and coins taped to it for phone calls?

R ____ Do you check under the car and car interior (front and rear) before entering?

S ____ When in your car, do you have a way of signaling for help?

T ____ Do you try not to walk alone?

U ____ When walking, do you wear non-restrictive shoes or clothing?

V ____ Do you avoid overloading yourself with packages when walking?

W ____ Do you wear highly-visible clothing when walking/jogging/biking, etc.?

X ____ Do you make it a rule never to hitchhike?

Y ____ Do you make it a rule never to pick up hitchhikers?

Z ____ Are you on the lookout for any problems that affect your neighborhood's safety?

____ TOTAL

Score: 0-13 = Safety Alert!
         14-26 = Uh-oh! Don't be so trusting!
         27-39 = You're doing well, but you can still fine-tune your safety skills!
         40-52 = Bravo! Keep up the good work!

BE SAFE!! DON'T BE A VICTIM!

SAFETY...
OUTSIDE THE HOME

I. PURPOSE:

To increase awareness of situations outside the home that require safety measures.

To increase safety skills outside the home.

II. GENERAL COMMENTS:

Safety comes first — but oftentimes when people are distracted, preoccupied or depressed, there is a tendency to overlook simple safety measures.

III. POSSIBLE ACTIVITIES: This handout can be used in conjunction with SAFETY INSIDE THE HOME (page 36).

A. 1. Distribute handouts.

2. Instruct group members to rate themselves on a scale of 0, 1, or 2. Then, total scores and refer to scoring guidelines on bottom.

3. Discuss with group members further explanations/examples:
    — When discussing D, *"Are you aware of high-risk and low-risk areas?"*, explore different situations, including:
      a) parking next to a van where undesirable characters might be
      b) dark, unsupervised areas
      c) outlying areas of parking lot
      d) unsafe neighborhoods
    — When discussing E, *"Would you be able to describe surroundings?"*, explore being on the lookout for abandoned cars, missing signs, reckless drivers, poor street lighting, etc.

4. Facilitate appropriate role-plays with the low-scoring responses.

5. Process benefits of activity.

B. 1. Distribute handouts.

2. Instruct group members to rate themselves on a scale of 0, 1, or 2. Then, total scores and refer to scoring guidelines on bottom.

3. Explain to group members that a basic skill for maintaining safety is the ability to accurately describe surroundings. Encourage group members to close their eyes and answer the following questions:
      a) How many people are in the room? What is the person on the right wearing? What is the person on the left's height, weight, hair color, skin color, and approximate age?
      b) How many exits are there in the room, and where are they?
      c) What are the general surroundings — furniture, lighting, noises, music, smells, etc.?

4. Show slides, pictures, or posters for 1-2 minutes and ask members to recall as many details as possible for an alternative/addition to this activity.

5. Evaluate and process with group members their abilities to describe surroundings and how this relates to safety.

My motto
that I live by...

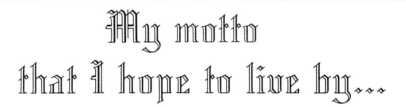

My motto
that I hope to live by...

My motto that I live by...

I. PURPOSE:

To promote a positive self-image by identifying mottos one lives by and hopes to live by.

II. GENERAL COMMENTS:

A motto is a brief sentence or phrase used to state what one believes in. A motto that one values can be a powerful way to strengthen self-identity and improve self-image.

III. POSSIBLE ACTIVITIES:

A. 1. Define "motto" and brainstorm several on chalkboard. Refer to the "MOTTO GAME", page 19, for a list of possible mottos.

2. Distribute handouts and instruct all group members to write, draw or symbolize a motto they live by, and hope to live by (without allowing others to see their papers). Group members' names should not be written on handout.
   Example.

   a. all for one and one for all.   b. one day at a time.

3. Post each member's handout around room in "gallery fashion".

4. Allow 5 minutes for members to browse.

5. Encourage group members to guess which motto belongs to each member. one-by-one, and then allow time for the originator to describe and discuss his/her thoughts.

6. Process benefits of identifying mottos.

B. 1. Discuss definition of motto, its impact on life-choices and decisions, and ultimately its effect on self-image.

2. Instruct all group members to write 3 mottos on separate strips of paper, and place in basket.

3. Taking turns, pass the basket so that all group members take one strip of paper. Instruct each group member to read the motto aloud, explain what it means to them, and possible influences on one's way of life.

4. Encourage all group members who *do* live by these mottos to share their insights.

5. Distribute handouts and instruct group members to write, draw or symbolize a motto they live by, and hope to live by. This can be done as an independent assignment if time does not permit in the group.

6. Process benefits of identifying mottos.

I ♡ Me

I. PURPOSE:

To identify positive, personal characteristics.

To increase self-esteem by receiving sincere compliments and positive feedback from others.

II. GENERAL COMMENTS:

Identifying positive characteristics one possesses and accepting positive feedback from others, can contribute to a healthy self-image and increase self-esteem. Focusing on one's strengths rather than weaknesses, will ultimately enhance performance in daily activities and improve relationships.

III. POSSIBLE ACTIVITIES:

A. 1. Introduce topics of self-image and self-esteem, with definitions from group members and facilitator's input as needed.

2. Distribute handouts and instruct each group member to write his/her name on the "collar" of the "I Love Me" shirt.

3. Pass papers around group circle so that each member has an opportunity to write 2 positive words, phrases, or sentences on each other's T-shirts (not in the heart-shaped space).

4. When each person receives own T-shirt, s/he is to write 5-10 positive characteristics in the heart-shaped space.

5. Share as a group, asking each member to stand and read all comments on T-shirt.

6. Give applause after each group member reads his/hers aloud.

7. Process benefits of this activity.

B. 1. Introduce topics of self-image and self-esteem, with definitions from group members and facilitator's input as needed.

2. Use this handout as a "good-bye" activity for an individual who is leaving the group or being discharged.

3. Ask the group member who is leaving, to have a "good-bye conversation" with facilitator in a separate room for approximately 10 minutes. At the same time, the group (and possibly a co-leader) completes the *I LOVE ME* handout by passing the paper around the group circle, so that each member has an opportunity to write 2 positive words, phrases or sentences about that person on the handout.

4. Invite the group member to rejoin the group when completed.

5. Pass the same paper around the room and instruct each group member to read aloud the comments that s/he wrote.

6. Provide an opportunity for the person who is leaving to reflect on his/her thoughts and feelings of the activity, including identifying his/her favorite comments.

7. Process benefits of giving and receiving compliments and how this affects self-image and self-esteem.

Make "Sense" of your ...

SELF-IMAGE

	SEE	HEAR	TASTE	SMELL	TOUCH

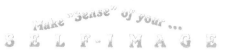
Make "Sense" of your ...
SELF-IMAGE

I. PURPOSE:

To identify various components that contribute to self-image.

To identify ways to self-nurture with appeal to the 5 senses.

II. GENERAL COMMENTS:

Self-image is how one "sees" or views oneself, and is affected by many factors. It can be influenced in a positive way when one is nurtured with enjoyable activities, experiences, and surroundings.

III. POSSIBLE ACTIVITIES:

A. 1. Introduce concept of self-image and how it relates to self-nurturance.

   2. Distribute handouts and explain as follows:

      a. In each block you are to write an activity, experience or surrounding which appeals to that particular sense and begins with the corresponding letter in the word "self-image". For example, using the letter E:

      SEE — evergreens
      HEAR — easy listening music
      TASTE — eating pizza
      SMELL — early morning coffee
      TOUCH — enjoying hugs

      b. When grid is complete, highlight those you are not presently incorporating into your lifestyle, but would like to in the future.

   3. Share responses as a group, setting goals as appropriate.

   4. Process benefits of self-nurturance.

B. 1. Introduce concept of self-image and how it relates to self-nurturance.

   2. Compile kit of sense-stimulators for "Self-Nurturing Party".

      e.g.   SEE   a. pictures (children playing, muted colors, outdoors, etc.)
                     b. clear container of sand
                     c. plant
                     d. stuffed animals
             HEAR   a. tape of different types of music (jazz, blues, classical, country, etc.)
                     b. radio/record player/compact disc player
                     c. ready-made tapes of environmental sounds
                     d. relaxation tapes
             TASTE a. cookies
                     b. fresh vegetables
                     c. fresh fruit
                     d. beverage
             SMELL a. spices/potpourri
                     b. aftershave/perfume
                     c. flowers
                     d. lemon
             TOUCH a. sheepskin
                     b. satin, silk, cotton
                     c. antiques
                     d. hand cream

   3. Distribute handouts.

   4. Introduce the sense of sight by encouraging group members to experience each sight stimulator from the kit.

   5. Instruct group members to jot down (in the SEE column) either the sense-stimulator from the kit, or their own ideas, which they find to be self-nurturing.

   6. Discuss and share as able.

   7. Proceed with the sense of hearing, the sense of taste, the sense of smell, and the sense of touch, as explained above in B.4-6.

   8. Process benefits of self-nurturance in conjunction with these five senses.

...grant me
the SERENITY
to accept the things
I cannot change...

_____

_____

_____

COURAGE to change
the things I can...

_____

_____

_____

and the WISDOM to
know the difference.

...grant me
   the SERENITY

I. PURPOSE:

To promote boundary recognition as a step to recovery.

II. GENERAL COMMENTS:

Tangible, concrete work with this theme reinforces its powerful message.

III. POSSIBLE ACTIVITIES:

A. 1. Distribute handouts.

2. Instruct group members to complete mini-posters with marking pens, paints, or crayons. (Completed works can be used for a cover of a folder, as a wall hanging in a room, or as an invitation for an upcoming event.)

3. Process the group by reinforcing the importance of the serenity theme.

B. 1. Distribute handouts.

2. Instruct group members to complete mini-posters with marking pens, paints, or crayons. (Completed works can be used for a cover of a folder, as a wall hanging in a room, or as an invitation for an upcoming event.)

3. Divide group into two subgroups.

4. Instruct one subgroup to list and discuss things (personal issues, topics, situations) they *cannot* change. As an additional activity for a future group, refer to WOULDA... SHOULDA... COULDA, page 13, using this *cannot change* list.

5. Instruct the second subgroup to list and discuss things (personal issues, topics, situations) they *can* change. As an additional activity for a future group, refer to original Life Management Skills, GOAL SETTING, pages 12-15, using this *can change* list.

6. Reconvene the group and share results.

7. Process benefits of this activity.

TOSSING that "OLD BAGGAGE"

"OLD BAGGAGE" refers to issues from the past which cannot be changed, accompanied by residual feelings. This "old baggage" consumes energy that might otherwise be used for self-improvement.

1) Specifically, write in your "old baggage" issues:

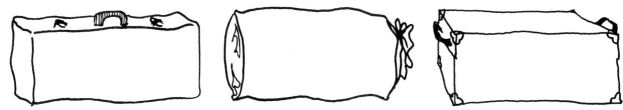

2) What is preventing you from getting rid of this "old baggage"?

_____

3) What are some ways you can resolve these past issues?

_____

4) What will you do with this extra energy after you've *tossed* your "old baggage"?

_____

Acknowledge EVERY Effort Towards Your Personal Growth!

I. PURPOSE:

To facilitate recovery by recognizing strong emotions from the past regarding things that cannot change.

To problem-solve methods of resolving past issues.

II. GENERAL COMMENTS:

Oftentimes, we are immobilized by events from the past. Many of these things we cannot change as noted in the SERENITY theme. Emotional energy needs to be free to work on other recovery issues.

III. POSSIBLE ACTIVITIES:

A. 1. Distribute handouts.

   2. Discuss topic, using content of first paragraph.

   3. Complete handouts, emphasizing need for support.

   4. Process benefits of this activity.

B. 1. Distribute handouts.

   2. Discuss topic, using content of first paragraph.

   3. Encourage group members to draw or make a collage of their "old baggage" on a separate piece of paper, using pictures or symbols, but no words.

   4. Ask group members to describe their "baggage" to the group as they are able, and one way they are considering resolving these issues.

   5. Complete handouts, emphasizing need for support.

   6. Process benefits of this activity.

BLACK | WHITE

BLACK and WHITE thinking leaves the whole world of GRAY out in the cold.
Try experimenting with gray thinking.

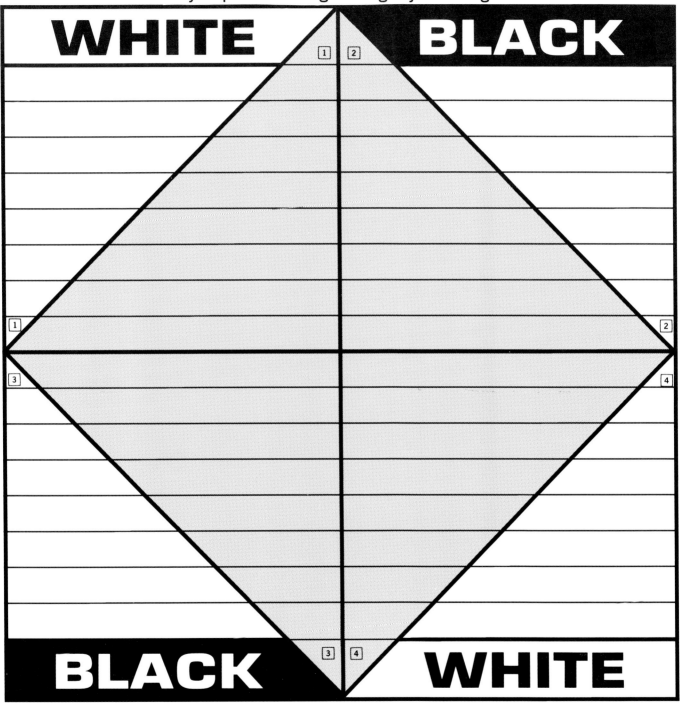

I. PURPOSE:

To facilitate recovery (1) by recognizing "absolute" or "all-or-nothing" statements, and (2) by learning how to neutralize them.

II. GENERAL COMMENTS:

"Black & white thinking" refers to "absolutes" or "all-or-nothing" statements. Many people in recovery work demonstrate "black & white thinking", and oftentimes extreme behavior is associated with this. Reframing the words or phrases, such as those noted on the handout, promotes neutralizing or blending of "black & white thinking" into "gray thinking".

III. POSSIBLE ACTIVITIES:

A. 1. Distribute handouts.

2. Explain topic with discussion of concept, including implications of "black & white thinking".

3. Instruct group members to write 4 examples of their own "absolutes" or "all-or-nothing" statements. Encourage group members to reframe those statements into neutral messages.
   e.g., absolute - "I hate myself when I goof up".
   neutral or gray - "I become impatient with myself at times".

4. Encourage group members to offer one example from their handouts to the group for feedback.

5. Process benefits of this activity.

B. 1. Before group, prepare card game by writing those "absolute" statements/phrases from bottom of handout several times each to make a deck of 30 cards.

2. Discuss concept of "black & white thinking", with group members eliciting personal examples.

3. Instruct each group member to choose a card and identify a time/situation in which s/he may use that statement/phrase, giving a specific example.

4. Ask group member to choose another member to reframe the "absolute" for him/her.

5. Continue until all have chosen a card and all group members have been asked to reframe.

6. Process benefits of identifying "black & white thinking" and receiving feedback on ways to reframe.

DO ANY OF THESE STRESSORS "HIT HOME"?

Day-to-day life has countless stressors. Identifying even the smallest irritant, as well as major life stressors, assists us in recognizing the amount of stress we actually encounter... and the VALUE of coping skills.

Stressors have a cumulative effect and can have unhealthy consequences relating to personal health, relationships, and all other life areas.

Check (✓) below the stressors you've experienced in the last few months.

- ☐ Your alarm clock not going off.
- ☐ Your favorite sports team losing.
- ☐ A recent illness.
- ☐ Dealing with bureaucracy/red-tape.
- ☐ A divorce.
- ☐ Losing a friend's long-distance phone number.
- ☐ Working with incompetent people.
- ☐ Not being able to find a kleenex... and needing it!
- ☐ Birth of a child.
- ☐ Being late on a deadline.
- ☐ Hearing disparaging comments about a minority.
- ☐ In-law problems.
- ☐ Spouse being under stress.
- ☐ Recent death of someone close to you.
- ☐ Having difficulty motivating yourself.
- ☐ Losing a game.
- ☐ Wanting to eat, but on a diet.
- ☐ Having only cold water for a bath.
- ☐ Spouse late coming home.
- ☐ Not being able to find the car keys.
- ☐ Anxiously awaiting a phone call.
- ☐ Late paying a bill.
- ☐ Someone telling you what to do.
- ☐ Moving to a new city.
- ☐ Not enough time for yourself.
- ☐ Having an empty gas tank and being in a rush.
- ☐ Sexual problems.
- ☐ Threat of war.
- ☐ Planning a large event.
- ☐ Being in trouble with the law.

- ☐ Anniversary of a beloved's death.
- ☐ Not having enough money to pay the bills.
- ☐ Parents treating you like a child.
- ☐ A new job.
- ☐ Someone telling you how to feel.
- ☐ Inability to conceive a child.
- ☐ Having no money and not wanting to borrow.
- ☐ Arguing with a good friend or relative.
- ☐ Out-of-town relatives staying with you.
- ☐ Spouse being too dependent on you.
- ☐ Seeing signs of aging in the mirror.
- ☐ Unwanted pregnancy.
- ☐ Not feeling well and not knowing why.
- ☐ Best friend asking to borrow money.
- ☐ An appliance/machine not working.
- ☐ Too much to do, not enough time.
- ☐ Someone canceling plans one-half hour before.
- ☐ Moving to a new house or apartment.
- ☐ Good friend feeling depressed.
- ☐ Someone telling you how to drive.
- ☐ Job interview.
- ☐ Boss putting pressure on you.
- ☐ Saying "yes" to too many things.
- ☐ Waiting in a long line.
- ☐ Being charged too much money.
- ☐ Electricity going out.
- ☐ Children not taking responsibility for themselves.
- ☐ _____
- ☐ _____
- ☐ _____

These stressors may not change, however your ability to "cope" with them CAN change!

STRESSORS "HIT HOME"?

I. PURPOSE:

To identify stressors as a first step in stress management.

II. GENERAL COMMENTS:

Common stressors are often overlooked and left unidentified. *Without identifying them, it is impossible to recognize the need for stress management.*

III. POSSIBLE ACTIVITIES:

A. 1. Facilitate discussion of stressors by brainstorming on a chalkboard.

2. Distribute handouts and instruct group members to follow directions.

3. Ask all group members to total checked boxes to compare numbers.

4. Encourage group members to discuss stress management techniques they have/can develop.

5. Process importance of recognizing potential stressors and ways to cope with them.

B. 1. Facilitate discussion of identifying stressors as a first step in stress management.

2. Distribute handouts and instruct group members to complete.

3. Review those checked. Ask group members which stressors they were surprised to see, or were unaware of, that contributed to their stress level. Discuss.

4. Encourage group members to discuss stress management techniques they have/can develop.

5. Process importance of recognizing potential stressors and ways to cope with them.

ANNOYANCES *STRESS* *IRRITANTS* *HASSLES*

PEEVES *ANNOYANCES*

HASSLES *IRRITANTS* *STRESS*

Don't sweat the "SMALL STUFF"

PEEVES

- Stressors come in all sizes and all forms . . .
   some are major life events . . .
   but MANY are everyday hassles . . .
   or . . . "small stuff".
- Effective coping skills can help to put these in perspective.

HASSLE / EXPERIENCE	MY REACTION	POSSIBLE COPING SKILLS
1.		
2.		
3.		

Don't sweat the
"SMALL STUFF"

I. PURPOSE:

To recognize the difference between major life stressors, and everyday hassles that create stress.

To develop an awareness of typical reactions to everyday hassles and identify more effective means to cope.

II. GENERAL COMMENTS:

Stress can come in all sizes and, if mismanaged, can have an unhealthy impact. Learning to gain control over the "small stuff" can contribute greatly to one's sense of wellness.

III. POSSIBLE ACTIVITIES:

A. 1. Generate discussion of varying degrees of stress, including group members' examples of major life stressors, as well as everyday hassles/annoyances/peeves/irritants.

2. Distribute handouts and instruct group members to complete.

3. Encourage each member to share his/her responses as time allows.

4. Formulate a list of "possible coping skills" on the chalkboard from all group members' responses. Add others as able.

5. Discuss wide range of options in coping with "small stuff".

6. Process benefits of this activity.

B. 1. Generate discussion of varying degrees of stress, including group members' examples of major life stressors, as well as everyday hassles/annoyances/peeves/irritants.

2. Discuss sources of stress, attempting to focus stress management in one category per group members' interests and needs,
        e.g.,   family,
               job,
               finances,
               time issues,
               internal messages,
               relationships, etc.

3. Decide on one category as a focus for this day's group. Use one example from the group on chalkboard,
        e.g.,   FAMILY

HASSLE/EXPERIENCE	MY REACTION	POSSIBLE COPING SKILLS
Sister never calls me, I always have to call her.	resentment, snippy answers	assertiveness
		don't call her for 2 weeks

4. Distribute handout, asking group members to complete handout with chosen category.

5. Pursue discussion of possible coping skills within that category.

6. Process benefits of this activity.

7. Choose additional categories for future groups sessions.

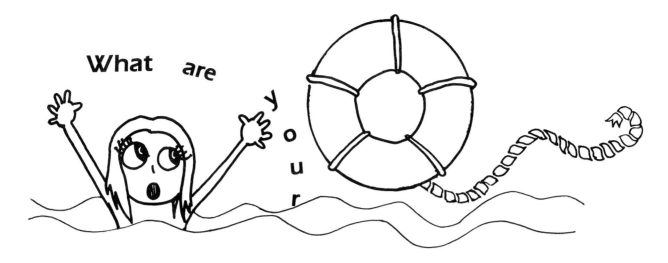

"LIFESAVERS"?

Who? Where? How?

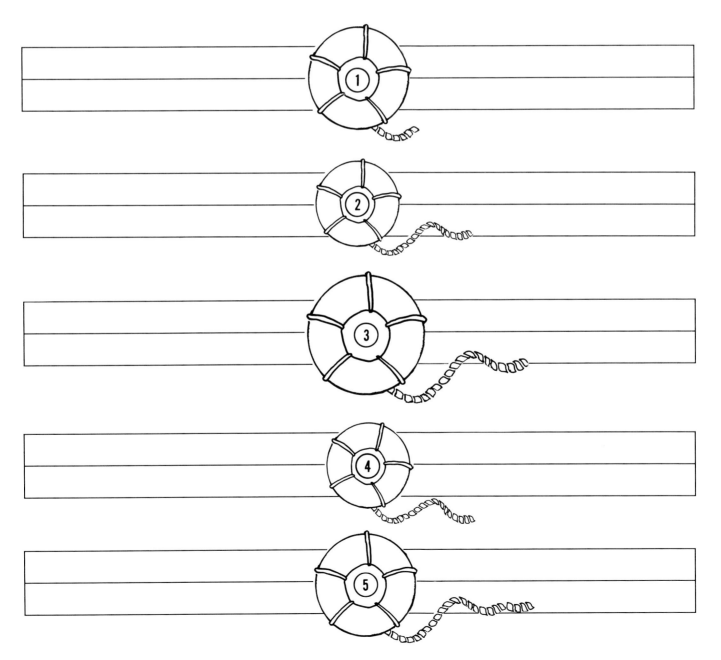

"LIFESAVERS"?

I. PURPOSE:

To identify various means of support.

To establish a plan to utilize designated support systems more effectively.

II. GENERAL COMMENTS:

Support systems are vital to an individual's well-being, however often are not established or utilized effectively. Individuals can increase their independence by knowing when and how to utilize these supports.

III. POSSIBLE ACTIVITIES:

A. 1. Introduce topic of "lifesavers" and support systems.

2. Brainstorm on chalkboard.

e.g. "LIFESAVERS"		Who? Where? How?
a good listener	(1)	husband, mother, sister
exercise, relaxation	(2)	health spa

3. Distribute handouts and encourage group members to complete.

4. Share responses as a group, focusing on goal setting.

5. Process benefits of this activity.

B. 1. Introduce topic of support systems.

2. Distribute 3 handouts to each group member.

3. Decide, as a group, on 3 categories of needs, e.g.,

physical	social
emotional	professional
spiritual	personal
intellectual	

4. Discuss each category, brainstorming on chalkboard as needed.

e.g., PHYSICAL

"LIFESAVERS"		Who? Where? How?
getting adequate sleep	(1)	ask my husband to watch the kids one morning each week.
taking breaks	(2)	explain to boss that I need to "walk away" from work sometimes.
crying	(3)	explain to children that crying is OK, so that I can cry in front of them.
exercising	(4)	join a community recreation center.
eating fresh fruits/vegetables	(5)	find a friend to go to the health food store with me.

Continue by discussing 2 remaining categories with examples.

5. Encourage group members to complete their 3 handouts.

6. Ask group members to share possible goals.

7. Process benefits of identifying various means of support.

#1 #1 #1 #1 #1 #1 #1 #1 #1 #1 #1 #1

We ALL have needs! It is important that each of us take responsibility for meeting these needs. It might be helpful to involve supports to assist us.

NEEDS:	Which of your needs are infringed on at times?	Why? When?	What are some ways to get these needs met?
PHYSICAL: (e.g. sleep, warmth, food, cleanliness)			
SOCIAL and BELONGING: (e.g. friends, affiliations, family)			
SELF-FULFILLMENT: (e.g. activities, accomplishments)			

It is almost impossible to meet others' needs if your needs aren't met first!

I. PURPOSE:

To increase support systems by identifying realistic ways to gain control in one's life.

II. GENERAL COMMENTS:

Socialized roles often prevent recognizing one's needs as #1. The self-perception "I am selfish and egotistical" can be restructured into "I have positive self-esteem and I am assertive".

III. POSSIBLE ACTIVITIES:

A. 1. Provide these examples of a modified Maslow's theory, or your own:

NEEDS:	Which of your needs are infringed upon?	Why? When?	What are some ways to get these needs met?
Physical:	eating nutritious meals	taking care of 1 year old	involve husband, talk to him, suggest late night dinners - *alone* with him!
Social and belonging:	going to church/temple	I have no transportation for special events.	call clergy and explain situation - ask for a ride.
Self-fulfillment:	art classes	no one to go with	get a friend to go with me/ decide to go by myself.

2. Request that each group member complete a handout and share as able.

3. Emphasize the choices available, but often unrecognized.

4. Discuss differences and similarities between group members, and the benefits of asserting the right to recognize our needs as important.

B. 1. Discuss concept of needs and needs-fulfillment.

2. Brainstorm on chalkboard examples of physical needs, social and belonging needs, and self-fulfillment needs.

3. Distribute handouts and instruct group members to complete.

4. Encourage discussion of individuals' completed handouts, providing feedback and support.

5. Process benefits of this activity.

For Your Information

As a newcomer to our program, we the _____ staff

at _____ would like to orient you to our schedule!

_____
_____
_____

_____
_____
_____

_____
_____
_____

_____
_____
_____

_____
_____
_____

_____
_____
_____

_____
_____
_____

_____
_____
_____

_____
_____
_____

_____
_____
_____

Hope your stay is comfortable!

I. PURPOSE:

To provide a quick, visual reference to daily activities.

To increase time management through scheduling of one's pertinent activities.

II. GENERAL COMMENTS:

A visual reminder of activities using the universal face of a clock can offer a much-needed schedule for clients/family members.

III. POSSIBLE ACTIVITIES:

A. 1. Complete first sentence on handout appropriately before distributing handouts to group members.

2. Encourage discussion of activities offered in the program, indicating recommended ones, as well as optional ones, for each individual.

3. Direct each group member to complete own handout by writing in the appropriate activities, times, and locations.

4. Process benefits of using this time management system.

B. 1. Use this handout in a one-to-one session to orient newcomers to a specific program.

2. Review schedule of activities offered in the program, for example:
meal times,
group activities,
medication times,
meeting times,
appointments,
etc.

3. Write in times, names of activities and locations.

4. Post completed form so that individual and significant other(s) will have easy access to the schedule.

5. Process benefits of using this time management system.

TIME MYTHOLOGY

Each of us has the same amount of time in each day, week, month, and year. How we *perceive* time, and how we prioritize tasks and spend our time, can differ greatly among us. Below are typical TIME-MYTHS, that create ineffective time management. Try to formulate a REALITY-STATEMENT to correspond with each TIME-MYTH. This will hopefully put things in perspective and help you to manage your time more effectively.

TIME-MYTHS

1. *"If I only had 2 more hours in each day, I'd be able to get it done."*

2. *"I'm waiting until I have more time."*

3. *"I never have time for the things I want to do."*

4. *"Time management is boring; it doesn't work for me."*

5. *"My time is not my own, and there's nothing I can do about it."*

6. *"I'm afraid I'll get too organized, and will lose my creativity."*

7. *"I need someone else to motivate me or I won't get it done."*

8. *"People keep interrupting me, so I can't get anything done."*

9. *"They have so much more time than I do!"*

10. *"There are not enough hours in the day."*

11. _____

REALITY-STATEMENTS

1. _____

2. _____

3. _____

4. _____

5. _____

6. _____

7. _____

8. _____

9. _____

10. _____

11. _____

Taking more control of your time, allows you more control of your life!

TIMΣ MΨTHOLOGΨ

I. PURPOSE:

To increase time management by recognizing typical unproductive, unreasonable, and/or overstated thoughts associated with time.

To increase time management by identifying reality-statements to offset typical time-myths.

II. GENERAL COMMENTS:

Frequently, time-myths hinder time management skills. These thoughts border on being irrational, and need to be put in perspective. Reality-statements provide a more rational approach to hopefully assist in managing time more effectively.

III. POSSIBLE ACTIVITIES: This handout can be used in conjunction with
TIME FOR TIPS & TIPS FOR TIME (page 50).

A. 1. Discuss concept of time-myths and their effects on time management.

2. Distribute handouts and review. Offer the 10 listed time-myths as examples of typical thoughts associated with time, encouraging group members to add others in appropriate spaces. Brainstorm on chalkboard as needed.

3. Instruct group members to complete handouts, giving this example of thoughts of your own:

TIME-MYTHS	REALITY-STATEMENTS
"If I only had 2 more hours"	"I have 24 hours each day to work with (just like everyone else), so I need to look at my priorities and begin scheduling my time accordingly."

4. Process benefits of this activity and discuss last statement on handout as a closure.

B. 1. Discuss concept of time-myths and their effects on time management. Read aloud first paragraph on handout.

2. Distribute blank sheets of paper and pencils.

3. Read aloud each time-myth, #1-10, asking group members to respond to the question:
    "When do you hear yourself saying this, or thinking this?"

Ask group members to write down their responses, trying to answer each one differently,
    e.g., Time-Myth: 1. when I am late in calling friends back
                2. whenever the topic of exercising comes up
                3. when I need more leisure time
                4. when I see those time management books at the library
                5. when friends ask me to socialize
                6. when creating at my drawing board
                7. when household tasks are waiting for me
                8. when I'm paying the bills
                9. when I look at single people's lifestyles
                10. at nighttime when I'm evaluating the day's accomplishments

4. Distribute handouts, instructing group members to complete by filling in their reality-statements.

5. Process benefits of this activity and discuss last statement on handout as a closure.

TIME for TIPS & TIPS for TIME

Review the following list and choose the tips that fit your particular time management needs! Remember to design an individualized time management system that fits your personality, so it will be more effective for you!

1. Be realistic with yourself regarding how much you can actually accomplish in a given time period.
_____

2. Realize that all tasks are not equally important and set priorities on a daily, weekly and/or monthly basis.
_____

3. Fine-tune your ability to say "NO" to additional responsibilities that infringe on your personal, work, and/or leisure time.
_____

4. Be aware of your peak energy periods and plan to do activities, which require a high level of concentration and performance, during those times.
_____

5. Ask yourself "What's the best use of my time right now?" and focus on that particular activity.
_____

6. Remember that striving for perfection takes time and usually isn't necessary. Complete tasks well enough to get the results you really need.
_____

7. Realize that many tasks/responsibilities can be delegated to others. Be sure to communicate your expectations clearly.
_____

8. Make basic decisions quickly to save energy for the more important and difficult decisions.
_____

9. Approach overwhelming responsibilities with a positive attitude, and learn to break large tasks into small, achievable ones.
_____

10. Make use of "waiting" time, by having small, uncomplicated tasks/activities to do... or simply plan to enjoy this time and relax.
_____

11. Request uninterruptible time whenever needed to achieve goals. Take control of your environment at home and/or work to establish a conducive place for task involvement and completion.
_____

12. Set goals and reward yourself when you've accomplished them.
_____

13. Always remind yourself of the benefits you'll derive from task completion.
_____

14. Free time, leisure activities, and exercise need to be scheduled/prioritized, as well as work activities.
_____

Circle three "tips for time" that you can incorporate into your individualized time management system:

1   2   3   4   5   6   7   8   9   10   11   12   13   14

GOAL Write one goal which needs attention now: _____
_____

A balanced lifestyle is a positive outcome of effective time management.

I. PURPOSE:

To identify components for an individualized time management system.

To establish one immediate time management goal.

II. GENERAL COMMENTS:

Effective time management is beneficial to self-esteem, relationships with others, life balance, and most all other aspects of life. By evaluating various time management tips, one can design an effective individualized time management system.

III. POSSIBLE ACTIVITIES: This handout can be used in conjunction with TIME MYTHOLOGY (page 49).

A. 1. Distribute handouts and discuss time management tips.

    2. Encourage group members to write, in the space provided, comments to assist them with their own personal situations.

    3. Elicit feedback from group on additional time management tips.

    4. Instruct group members to set appropriate goals.

    5. Process benefits of effective time management.

B. 1. Distribute handouts and discuss time management tips.

    2. Distribute a blank card to each group member.

    3. Instruct him/her to write one time management tip s/he would like to share with the group. e.g., making lists before going grocery shopping.

    4. Collect, put in basket, and instruct group members to choose one (not their own) and read aloud.

    5. Distribute handouts, and complete.

    6. Compare group's time management tips with those on handout.

    7. Process by asking group members to name one time management tip they plan to use.

FEEDBACK-LIFE MANAGEMENT SKILLS II

Check the topics that were of special interest in Life Management Skills II:

- ☐ Activities of Daily Living
- ☐ Anger Management
- ☐ Assertion
- ☐ Communication: Verbal
- ☐ Communication: Nonverbal
- ☐ Coping Skills
- ☐ Grief/Loss
- ☐ Humor
- ☐ Life Balance
- ☐ Money Management
- ☐ Parenting
- ☐ Reminiscence
- ☐ Safety Issues
- ☐ Self-Esteem/Self-Image
- ☐ Steps to Recovery
- ☐ Stress Management
- ☐ Support Systems
- ☐ Time Management

Check the topics which would be of interest in future publications:

- ☐ Addictive Behavior Issues
- ☐ Aging
- ☐ Behavior Modification
- ☐ Creative Expression
- ☐ Eating Disorders
- ☐ Forms/Charts
- ☐ Job Readiness - Prevocational
- ☐ Reality Orientation
- ☐ Relapse Prevention
- ☐ Relationships
- ☐ Self-Empowerment
- ☐ Sex-Role Stereotyping
- ☐ Sexual Issues
- ☐ Other _____
  _____
  _____
  _____
  _____

What pages would you like to have in a 24" x 36" laminated poster? _____
_____
_____

Is there a specific population you'd like addressed in future publications? _____

Comments on LMS II: _____
_____
_____

Can this comment be published as an attestation? _____

_____
Signature

Name _____	Title _____
Facility _____	Occupation _____
Address _____	Home Address _____
City _____	City _____
State _____ Zip _____	State _____ Zip _____
Phone (work) (___) _____	Phone (home) (___) _____

(SEE REVERSE SIDE FOR ORDER FORM)

Multiple products are available in Sets, Kits, Packages, or Paks to offer integrated programming.

LMS BOOK SET - 2 books

	Your Price
Life Management Skills	$ 34.95
Life Management Skills II	$ 34.95
TOTAL	$~~69.90~~ $65.00

LMS II KIT - 1 book / cards

Life Management Skills II	$ 34.95
Self-Manager II cards	$ 13.00
TOTAL	$~~47.95~~ $45.00

TRI-RESOURCE KIT - 1 book / 1 poster / 1 game

Life Management Skills	$ 34.95
Emotions poster	$ 12.50
Bridge of Self-Confidence game	$ 49.95
TOTAL	$~~97.40~~ $90.00

PROGRAM PACKAGE - 2 books / 1 poster / BSC game & cards

Life Management Skills	$ 34.95
Life Management Skills II	$ 34.95
Emotions poster	$ 12.50
Bridge of Self-Confidence game	$ 49.95
Self-Manager II cards	$ 13.00
TOTAL	$~~145.35~~ $135.00

POSTER PAK - 8 posters + 1 free
Choose any 8 posters, get 9th one free!

	$ 12.50
	x 9
TOTAL	$~~112.50~~ $100.00

SHIPPING AND HANDLING

TOTAL	US	Canada**	Foreign**
$0 - 34.99	$ 3.00	$ 6.25	$ 21.75
$35 - 69.99	6.00	11.25	39.50
$70 - 104.99	8.75	16.25	56.25
$105 - 139.99	11.50	21.25	75.00
$140 - 174.99	14.25	26.25	90.50
$175 - 209.99	17.00	31.25	106.00
$210 and up	19.75	36.25	116.50

	Canada & Foreign
	** Please remit in US Funds only. If shipping & handling costs exceed or are less than chart, adjustment(s) will be made.

Allow 2-4 weeks for delivery.

FAX 216/831-1355
216/831-9209 • 800/669-9208

Check or purchase order required. Fax us your P.O. for quick service!

PLEASE SEND ME:

___ *Life Management Skills* book	@ $ 34.95	$ ___
___ *Life Management Skills II* book	@ $ 34.95	$ ___
___ *Bridge of Self-Confidence game*	@ $ 49.95	$ ___
___ *Frese Videotape*	@ $ 69.95	$ ___

Multiple Products:

___ LMS Book Set (2 books)	@ $ 65.00	$ ___
___ LMS II Kit (1 book / cards)	@ $ 45.00	$ ___
___ Tri-Resource Kit (1 book / 1 game / 1 poster)	@ $ 90.00	$ ___
___ Program Package (2 books / 1 poster / BSC game & cards)	@ $135.00	$ ___
___ Poster Pak (8 posters + 1 free = 9 posters)	@ $100.00	$ ___

Posters:

___ Black & White Thinking	___ Emotions	@ $ ___
___ Food Group Review	___ emotions (French)	@ $ ___
___ Look For Alternatives	___ Emociones (Spanish)	@ $ ___
___ Positive Problem Solving	___ Emozioni (Italian)	@ $ ___
___ Right To Change	___ Emotionen (German)	@ $ ___
___ Self-Esteem Boosters & Busters	___ Hargashot (Hebrew w/o vowels)	@ $ ___
___ Serenity	___ Hargashot (" w / vowels & English)	@ $ ___
___ To Risk or Not to Risk		

TOTAL POSTERS ___ each @ $ 12.50   SUBTOTAL $ ___

The following BSC game components can be ordered separately.

___ A-Z reference guide★	★ All included in		
___ Emotions reference guide★		@ $ 2.50	$ ___
___ A-Z cards★	*Bridge of*	@ $ 3.50	$ ___
___ Emotions cards★	*Self-Confidence Game*	@ $ 5.00	$ ___
___ Self-Manager I cards★		@ $ 7.00	$ ___
___ Self-Manager II cards (not included in BSC game)		@ $ 13.00	$ ___
		@ $ 13.00	$ ___

Shipping and Handling (see chart on left) ___
Ohio residents only, add 7% sales tax ___

TOTAL $ ___

*** If tax exempt, please send copy of tax exemption certificate*

Make checks payable to: **WELLNESS REPRODUCTIONS INC.**
23945 Mercantile Road, Suite 400
Beachwood, Ohio 44122-5924

SHIP TO:

Name _____

Title / Occupation _____

Facility _____

Address _____

City _____ State _____ Zip _____

Phone [___]

For further mailings — home address if different from shipping address:

Address _____

City _____ State _____ Zip _____

Phone [___]